A WORLD

OF

MANCHESTERS

A WORLD OF

MANCHESTERS

ROY COOKSON

A FASCINATING GUIDE TO ALL THE VILLAGES,
TOWNS AND CITIES THROUGHOUT THE WORLD
NAMED MANCHESTER

CASTHERMEN

First published in England in 2002
by
Casthermen Books
44 Austin Drive,
Didsbury,
Manchester, M20 6EG
0161 434 2872

A catalogue record for this book is available from the British Library

ISBN 0 9542404 0 5

Front cover illustration by Leslie Bickerton

This book was designed, printed and bound by the author at the Manchester
School of Printing, City College, Wythenshawe whilst a student on the
Introduction to Printing and Graphic Communications Course. This would
not have been possible without the help and guidance of Bob Downing, Head
of the Print Department and his staff, in particular Simon Hirst, Denis
Kenny, Malcolm Yates and David Gaskill, also Bill Parker and the staff of
the College Reprographic Department and the staff of the College Resource
Centre. To all of whom, and my fellow students, I extend my heartfelt
thanks.

CONTENTS

CONTENTS

A WORLD OF MANCHESTERS

AUTHOR'S NOTE

In preparing this book I have attempted in the interest of cohesion to give the same type of information for each Manchester; the location, population, a brief history and so on. This format has been followed wherever possible. However for some Manchesters my source of information has been full to overflowing whilst for others it has been difficult to obtain anything but the basic facts. The many kind people who have taken the time and trouble to answer my letters of enquiry have provided much of the information. Altogether I have written nearly two hundred letters, sent numerous emails and made countless telephone calls. I have also made full use of libraries, especially the Manchester Central Reference Library and the British Museum Library in London. I have found the Internet a most useful (if at times frustrating!) method of obtaining information.

Whilst on holiday in the USA I took the opportunity to continue my research in the San Francisco Library and the Chamber of Commerce, much to the chagrin of my wife who, naturally, wanted to see the sights! I'm happy to report that we managed to do both. I make no claim to have listed all Manchesters in the world as, doubtless, some readers may know of one or more that I have not found. If so please contact me through the publishers as I would wish to incorporate new information in a future edition.

My thanks go to all my correspondents; to the patient library staff who went to endless trouble on my behalf; to my Internet contacts and to the countless other people who in one way or another have helped me, many of whom I am now pleased to call friends. With these, I must include my fellow students and staff at the Manchester School of Printing at the City College and the Reprographic Department staff who helped me every step of the way in learning how to design, print and bind this book. I was the oldest student by far and enjoyed every minute of the course. Finally, my grateful thanks to Leslie Bickerton for the cover design and several illustrations, and to my friend Tom Tudor for proof reading, without flinching, my unique version of the English language and its grammar. Lastly, and most importantly, to my wife, Norma, for her constant support and encouragement without which I would have given up years ago. All errors and omissions are my own.

CW01499571

Roy Cookson
Manchester, England,
2002

1

A WORLD OF MANCHESTERS

INTRODUCTION

The British Empire, at its zenith, comprised of upwards of a quarter of the world's peoples and one fifth of the earth's land surface. The sun, if not finally set on the greatest empire the world has ever known (as there are still tiny pockets here and there) is well down on the horizon. The most enduring legacy of this great empire is the widespread use of the English language, today truly the world's lingua franca. However, the many hundreds of thousands of emigrants who left these shores to build a new life in the colonies took with them much more than their language and a few personal possessions. Their culture and customs were as much a part of their "baggage" as their language. The emigrants' memories of their homeland remained strong and were reflected in many ways, not least being in the naming of the places in which they came to settle. Thus today, throughout the world, one comes across English, Irish, Welsh and Scottish place names. They provided a poignant reminder of home to the hardy souls who travelled to the outposts of Empire in search of fame or fortune, or to escape a life of unremitting hardship, a common experience for most of the working class. Some left their mother country in chains as criminals and chose to remain to make a new life in the colonies once their sentences had been served.

Many of these early settlements were transitory in nature, being deserted once the local timber or mineral deposits had been exhausted, and their names died with them. Others survived and flourished and many great towns and cities throughout the world still proudly bear the name first given by their pioneering settlers. Even in these post-Empire days it is amazing how many of these names have been retained and many British villages, towns and cities have their namesakes in distant parts of the world and none more so than the great city of Manchester.

That North America should have the lion's share of Manchesters is not surprising, being a consequence of the large emigration to America from the north of England and the strong links, through the cotton industry, between Manchester, England and the southern states of the USA. In the mid-nineteenth century when Manchester was at its zenith, the city was much admired throughout the world. It was a pioneering city, the world's first industrial city, "Cottonopolis" as it came to be known, and was undoubtedly one of the richest cities on any continent in Victorian times. Some of the new Manchesters founded in distant lands were so named in the hope that they would eventually emulate the success of the original Manchester in England.

In general it was in the virgin territories of North America, more particularly in what became the United States, that new settlements were given names from the immigrants' home countries. The contrast between Canada and the USA is striking, with Canada having but two Manchesters

A WORLD OF MANCHESTERS

INTRODUCTION

(as far as I have been able to discover) and a Lake Manchester named as recently as 1947, compared with the USA's fifty plus. In view of the waves of emigrants who left these shores to find a new life south of the equator, it is surprising that Manchester is not a commonplace name in Australia or New Zealand. In spite of the most diligent of searches I have not discovered any village or town named Manchester in Australia, only a Manchester Square and a Manchester Lake, and but a single Manchester in New Zealand (and that a homestead). A glance at a map of either country will reveal many other British place names with towns in Yorkshire being particularly well represented. Why this should be so I have no explanation other than there was (and is) a link through the wool trade to Yorkshire and no true Yorkshireman would name a place after a town in Lancashire! There may also have been a tendency to adopt, or adapt, the original Aboriginal or Maori place name rather than import a European name, although this doesn't explain why other British towns and cities have their counterparts in the antipodes but not Manchester.

In India, and to a lesser extent, other parts of the British Empire, the countries were already well populated by the indigenous peoples and the existing place names were often retained when the first European settlers arrived. South Africa, in addition to its proud native population, also had other European settlers, mainly Dutch, with whom the British fought to gain control of the region. Hence, it is perhaps not so surprising that I have been unable to find any Manchesters, apart from farm names, in the many parts of Africa that were coloured pink on the world maps of empire, or on the Indian sub-continent. Whether any ever existed and failed to survive or had their names changed, as has often happened, I cannot say. However, other British towns have their namesakes in these former dominions and colonies so why not Manchester?

Apart from the countries already mentioned I came across Manchesters in the Caribbean (Jamaica) and, remarkably, in Bolivia. Recently I also came across a Manchester on a map of Suriname (formerly Dutch Guiana). Suriname has not proved to be the easiest of countries to get to know and, in spite of my most determined efforts, I have been unable to make contact. However, I will persevere with my enquiries. I feel certain that there are other places, perhaps too small to be shown on maps or mentioned in reference books, which carry the proud name of Manchester. Rather like the painting of the Forth Bridge, my search is unending.

INTRODUCTION

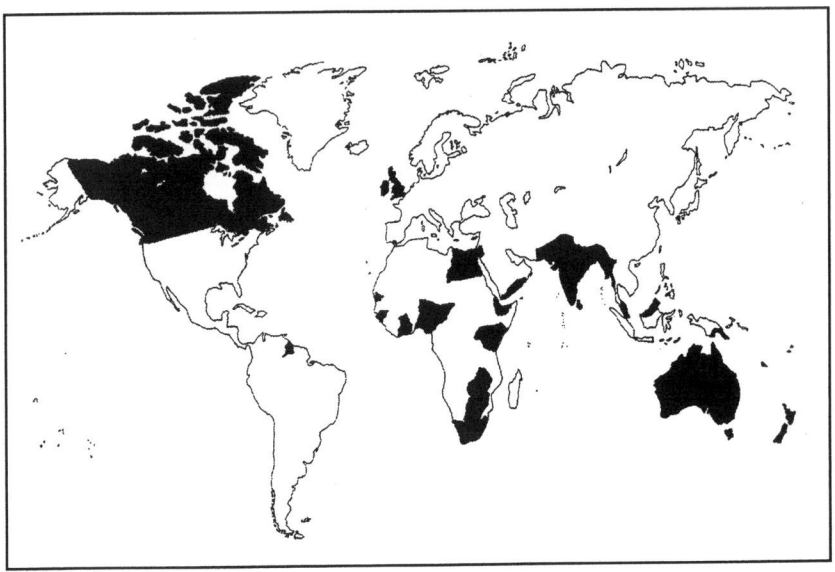

"The Empire on which the Sun Never Set"

The map shows the British Empire in 1897 at the time of the Diamond Jubilee of Queen Victoria, the "Queen Empress". There were innumerable small islands dotted about the world, particularly in the Pacific, which were part of the Empire but are not shown on the map. With the acquisitions gained at the end of the First World War in 1918 the Empire encompassed over a quarter of the world's population and a fifth of the land area.

MANCHESTER, ENGLAND
'The Capital of the North'

Location   Latitude 53.30N. Longitude 2.15W.
The major city of northwest England. A regional financial centre and the hub of a large urban/industrial conurbation.

Population City of Manchester 439,549 (2000). Greater Manchester conurbation 2,585,700 (2000). Population within 30-mile radius 6,296,721

It is said that the Austrian Emperor, Joseph II, once complained to Mozart that the great maestro's music contained "too many notes". I have some sympathy with the Emperor. Manchester has too much history, far too much to do it justice in a few paragraphs. However, in keeping with the general format of this book, that is what I have attempted. For brevity's sake I have had to be selective and many significant events and people get only a passing mention – and some no mention at all. For the reader who rightly thinks, "But what about so-and-so?" my apologies; each omission caused me pain.

The first Manchester, "the original and still the best" as its citizens vouchsafe, owes its origin and name to the siting of a Roman fort on a low sandstone plateau on the confluence of the rivers Medlock and Irwell. The timber palisade fort was erected between AD76-86 although there is evidence of an earlier Celtic settlement on the site. The Romans named the fort Mamucium from the Celtic word "mamma" which described the breast-like rounded hill on which the fort was built.

Over the next two centuries a civilian settlement grew around the wooden fort (later rebuilt in stone) which included houses for artisans and merchants. The fort served as a military staging post for legionaries marching between Eboracum (York) and Deva (Chester) and those on their way to and from Luguvalium (Carlisle) for or after garrison duty on Hadrian's Wall. The name Manchester came much later, long after the departure of the Romans, with "chester" from the Old English ceaster (Latin "castra" - camp) indicating it was once a Roman settlement. It is fitting that the first Manchester should have a name partly derived from the word breast as the city has mothered a family of over fifty daughter Manchesters throughout the world.

After the departure of the Romans in the fourth century, the site of Manchester appears to have been deserted for several hundred years. By the ninth century there is evidence of a Saxon settlement in the area and in 919 the West Saxon king Edward the Elder (son of Alfred the Great) sent men to "Mameceaster" to repair and man the fort. The Saxon settlement was about a mile upstream from the site of the Roman fort and it is likely that it was from this settlement that present day Manchester grew.

MANCHESTER, ENGLAND

The site of Manchester formed part of the lands (known as the Salford Hundreds) granted by King William 1 to Roger de Poitevin who had fought for William at the Battle of Hastings in 1066. Roger de Poitevin, in turn, subdivided his land between his followers and thus Albert de Grelley became the first baron of Manchester. The town (or village as it was) was mentioned in the Domesday Book in 1086 AD. This was a survey of his new kingdom carried out on the orders of King William 1 (William the Conqueror). The Domesday Book's entry under the Royal Manor of Salford reads: *"the church of St. Mary and the church of St. Michael held in Mameceaster one curacate of land quit from every due except geld"*.

Manchester was a very small agricultural settlement at the time of the Domesday Book surrounded by forest and wasteland. It remained so throughout the eleventh and twelfth centuries but by the thirteenth century a weekly market was being held on Saturdays. In 1227 the right to hold an annual fair was granted by the Lord of the Manor. Town life began to develop and in 1301 the fledgling town was granted its first Charter. Though it was to suffer grievously from the Black Death in 1351, (as it was to suffer from further plagues in years to come), Manchester grew steadily in local importance, especially after woollen and linen industries were introduced from Flanders.

During the sixteenth century the name Manchester came into common usage, a corruption of the Old English Mameceaster. By the time of the outbreak of the Civil War (1642-1652), in which the citizens of Manchester resisted a Royalist siege, the town was flourishing becoming an important market for cloths made in the surrounding hamlets and towns. Manchester merchants exported these cloths to Europe via London where there was a Manchester Hall in the cloth market, which dealt in Lancashire goods.

The generally damp climate of the area benefited the weaving of fustian, a cloth with a linen warp and a cotton weft, which was introduced circa 1620. This in turn led in the 18th and 19th centuries to the development of Manchester as the leading centre in the world for the manufacture of cotton textiles. Daniel Defoe, journalist and author of "Robinson Crusoe", described Manchester in 1726 as being, *"the greatest mere village in England where the grand manufacture is that of cotton in all its varieties"*

The 1745 Rebellion saw Bonnie Prince Charlie stopping off in Manchester en-route to London to claim the crown, only to turn back at Derby before being finally defeated at the battle of Culloden (1746). He lodged at the Bull's Head tavern in the centre of Manchester (destroyed by bombs in the Second World War blitz of 1940). A small number of local men joined up with the Prince forming the "Manchester Regiment", most meeting with death or imprisonment as a result of the defeat of Charles.

MANCHESTER, ENGLAND

The coming of the Canal Age after 1760 further opened up Manchester's trade, the canal link with the port of Liverpool being of particular importance. It became an artery through which raw cotton was imported and finished products exported, though much of the trade between the two cities continued to be carried by road wagons. The city's first cotton mill was erected in the early 1770s. With the advent of steam power, aided by the availability of large coal deposits in the area, by 1830 nearly a hundred mills were operating in Manchester, with many more throughout southeast Lancashire. The world's first passenger steam railway (of George Stephenson and "Rocket" fame) opened in 1830 linking Manchester and Liverpool and the subsequent railway mania saw the town linked by rail with most other parts of Britain by the 1850's.

In 1819 a peaceful demonstration for parliamentary reform held on St. Peter's Field, near the centre of the town, resulted in eleven deaths and hundreds injured when magistrates ordered the yeomanry to disperse the crowd. This event gained the name "Peterloo Massacre" in mocking analogy to the recent defeat of Napoleon's army at the battle of Waterloo (1815). Such was the reaction to this slaughter that for some time there was a fear of revolution in the air and soldiers were stationed throughout the town.

Parliamentary Reform in 1832 led to demands for municipal reform and, in the face of much entrenched opposition, Manchester was granted a Charter of Incorporation in 1838. Even after the granting of Incorporation the fight for the control of the town continued, the former Police Commissioners refusing to give up control of the Town Hall to the new Borough Council. It took a further Act of Parliament in 1842 and the purchase, for £200,000, of the Manorial Rights of the Mosley family before the citizens of Manchester truly controlled their own town. During the first half of the nineteenth century the town enjoyed an unprecedented expansion of industry and growth of population. The population, which had numbered about 10,000 in 1717, climbed to more than 300,000 by 1850. Manchester was the world's first industrial city and became the cradle of an industrial revolution that was to change the very face of the earth.

Undoubtedly the mid 19th century was Manchester's "Golden Age", the city becoming a world leader not only in commerce and industry, but also in intellectual and cultural life. The Chartists (1838-1850s), a movement in favour of universal manhood suffrage and other parliamentary reforms, received massive support in Manchester and the surrounding cotton towns, as did the Anti-Corn Law League formed at the same time. This movement for free trade was organised and directed by Richard Cobden and John Bright largely from its Manchester headquarters. A "Free Trade Hall" was erected in 1840 on St. Peter's Fields, the site of the Peterloo Massacre, as a venue

MANCHESTER, ENGLAND

for meetings of the League. The magnificent Free Trade Hall, which still graces the city (though soon to be "redeveloped" as a hotel), was built in 1853 on the site of the earlier hall. This hall, rebuilt after being largely destroyed by the German Luftwaffe in the Second World War, remains a lasting symbol of this era in the history of the city. In the same year Queen Victoria conferred the title of "city" on Manchester, giving due recognition of its growing national and international importance.

The old ....   and the new.......
Manchester Cathedral 1756   The Bridgewater Hall 1996

The "Manchester School" of liberal economic thought was immensely influential both in England and abroad throughout the second part of the nineteenth century. The "Manchester Guardian" newspaper, (founded 1821, renamed "The Guardian" in 1959), achieved national and world eminence, as did the Halle Orchestra founded in 1858 and still going strong. Friedrich Engels, one of the founding fathers of communism, based his book "The Condition of the Working Class in England" (1845) on his experience in Manchester. Owens College, now the Victoria University of Manchester, opened in 1851 and John Dalton (1776-1844) was to develop his atomic theory, the foundation of modern chemistry, at the college.

The overwhelming importance of overseas trade in the life of the city led to the opening of the Manchester Ship Canal by Queen Victoria in 1894. This canal, a marvel of Victorian engineering, gave ocean going ships access

MANCHESTER, ENGLAND

to the very heart of the industrial conurbation of south east Lancashire and made Manchester the world's biggest inland port. That the nineteenth century was a time of great confidence in the city's future was reflected by the erection of fine public and commercial buildings. The grandest was, and still is today, the magnificent Neo-Gothic Town Hall opened in 1877.

Manchester Town Hall

Designed by Alfred Waterhouse it is considered by many to one of the finest public buildings in the country. The lavish interior bears a striking resemblance to that of the Palace of Westminster in London and has been used by television and film companies as a "stand in" for Sir Charles Barry's famous Parliament building.

By the end of the nineteenth century the character of the city had changed. Manufacturing had diversified out of cotton into engineering including the manufacture of steam engines, locomotives, armaments and machine tools. The city also developed a strong commercial presence becoming the regional centre for warehousing, banking and finance. In the Manchester Stock Exchange (the "Royal Exchange", now a theatre), the yarns and cloths of the world were bought and sold. This diversification, which continued into the early part of the twentieth century, included Britain's embryo car industry when Ford opened a plant in Trafford Park, the largest industrial estate in the world at the time.

MANCHESTER, ENGLAND

The end of the First World War, in which the men and women of Manchester played a heroic part, marked the beginning of the decline of the city from its mid Victorian peak. However, in 1931, Manchester, which had steadily extended its boundaries over the years, again demonstrated faith in its future with the incorporation of the new garden suburb of Wythenshawe within the city boundaries. This was the largest concentration of municipal housing in the world at the time and in many ways served as the model for other council housing estates throughout the country.

The decline of the cotton industry and the world wide economic slump of the 1930s took their toll. Even in this dark economic period the citizens of Manchester looked to the future with the opening, in 1934, of the Central Reference Library with its impressive circular reading room. This library (pictured below) through its various specialist sections, including the world famous Henry Watson Music Library, serves the needs of academics, business people and general readers not just in Manchester but also throughout the north west of England and beyond. It is still, without question, one of the major reference libraries in Britain today.

The Second World War hit Manchester hard with considerable damage being caused by bombing. In the Christmas blitz of 1940 large parts of the city centre were destroyed. After the Second World War economic decline continued with manufacturing industry giving way to commercial activity as the main source of employment.

Manchester Central Reference Library

A WORLD OF MANCHESTERS

MANCHESTER, ENGLAND

In the immediate post war period a massive housing regeneration programme was undertaken with major slum clearance schemes in the inner city and new housing developments on the outskirts, particularly in north Cheshire. Although there has been considerable post war immigration into the city from Commonwealth countries, particularly the West Indies and the Indian subcontinent, the population of the city has fallen steadily from its peak of 766,300 in 1931 to its present figure of 439,549.

Manchester is still vibrant and go ahead and can rightly claim to be Britain's second city and "the capital of the north". The city now has four universities; an international airport voted "the world's favourite" in 1996; new concert and exhibition halls and world famous football teams in Manchester United and Manchester City. The City Fathers are making strenuous efforts to regenerate the city and the redesign and rebuilding of the city centre is virtually complete, made all the more necessary by the extensive damage caused by an I.R.A bomb in 1996. Although the bid to host the Olympic Games in the year 2000 was unsuccessful, the city was selected as the venue for the Commonwealth Games of 2002, for which a new state-of-the-art stadium has been built on the eastern side of the city. Manchester can look forward to the twenty first century with great pride in its past and growing confidence in its future.

Transport links

Road	At centre of major motorway network – M56/M61/M62 to M6 (north/south). M60 (Manchester outer ring motorway) to M56 (west), M62 (East). Numerous other motorway links within Greater Manchester.
Rail	Extensive network of local and long distance rail links. Metrolink Rapid Light Transport system links Bury with Altrincham via Manchester city centre. Planned to be extended to other areas.
Water	Manchester Ship Canal, 36 miles in length, giving sea-going vessels direct access to the city. Now little used for commercial traffic. The extensive network of eighteenth and nineteenth century narrow boat canals is being restored, mainly for recreational use.
Air	Manchester International Airport (10 miles) – worldwide scheduled and charter flights - direct rail link to airport.
Climate	Manchester is famous for its rain. A temperate climate with mild, wet winters; summers variable.
Post codes	(Greater Manchester) - M followed by individual digit/letter code.
Local Press	"Manchester Evening News", Deansgate, Manchester. (daily),

MANCHESTER, ENGLAND

"Manchester Metro" (weekly) and various other local weekly papers.
References   "Rich Inheritance" Ed. N.J.Frangopulo, S.R.Publishers, 1969.
"Manchester" Alan Kidd "Town & City" Series, Ryburn Publishing, Keele University Press.

G.Mex – the old Central Railway Station has gained
a new lease of life as an exhibition hall

The Venice of the North? Not quite! The River Irwell
in the centre of Manchester

MANCHESTER, ENGLAND

Abraham Lincoln keeps a fatherly eye on the city
from his plinth in Lincoln Square

As does Prince Albert, Queen Victoria's Consort,
from his lofty perch opposite the Town Hall

THE AMERICAS

"In fourteen ninety two, Columbus sailed the Ocean Blue"

The simple rhyme above has been taught to countless generations of schoolchildren, the author included, as an easy way to remember the date of the discovery of the "New World" of America. However, later research credits the Viking Leif Ericson as being the first European to set foot in North America, circa 1000AD. The Vikings named the new land "Vinland" after the grapes and vines they found there. To confirm the Viking presence archaeologists have uncovered the remains of a Viking settlement in Newfoundland.

It strikes me as rather odd to use the words "discover" or "discovery" in relation to the early European voyages to America as both North and South America were richly populated long before the Europeans appeared on the scene. They were more journeys of exploration and conquest than discovery, which subsequently led to the subjugation of the indigenous peoples and the settlement of their lands by European immigrants. The story of many of these journeys of exploration and the hardships faced by the early European settlers is a fascinating one and therefore, where possible, I have included a brief outline of the exploration and early settlement of each area in which there is a Manchester. I have set out the Manchesters of the Americas in alphabetical order from Bolivia to the United States. I was as surprised to find a Manchester in Bolivia (and in Suriname), as I was to find so many in the United States. Most States in the USA have a Manchester, some two or three!

Home from home in North America!
(Picture courtesy of Manchester Development Authority, Georgia)

THE AMERICAS

South America showing Bolivia and Suriname

Landlocked Bolivia - Manchester lies in the far north
Pando Region where many rivers feed the mighty Amazon.

BOLIVIA
MANCHESTER (Pando District)

Location   Latitude 11.33S. Longitude 68.04W.
In the Pando District in extreme northeast corner of Bolivian Amazonia.

Population 10,000 (estimated by Bolivian Embassy) – this appears to be a very high estimate as figures produced by the 1992 Census give the population of the whole Pando region as only 40,000.

A passing mention in a reference book of a Manchester in Bolivia led me into one of the most intensive pieces of detective work I have had to undertake in the preparation of this book. Because of its remote location, deep in the Bolivian Amazon, even to verify the existence of a Manchester in this South American Republic proved extraordinarily difficult.

Having exhausted all local sources of information my search took me to the British Museum Library in London and to contact with the Bolivian Embassy (who were unaware that they had a Manchester until they checked!). I spent endless unrewarding hours on the Internet and reading every reference book on Bolivia that I could lay my hands on. I enlisted the support of Father Bill Murphy, a Roman Catholic priest working in Bolivia, but even he, from within the country, found it impossible to obtain detailed information on Manchester. The rather sketchy story that I finally pieced together is one of Victorian enterprise by a native born Mancunian who set out to make his fortune on the other side of the world.

Anthony Webster James, a metallurgical engineer, born in Manchester, England, arrived in Bolivia in 1885 to work in Potosi, the site of the legendary silver mines. Potosi is one of the highest cities in the world (13,780ft.) and in the late 16th and early 17th centuries was the main source of the world's silver. In association with the tycoon Simon Patino (known as the Tin King and founder of Rio Tinto Zinc), he later established a rubber smelter for the then thriving local rubber industry in the remote northern Pando region. A workers' settlement grew up around the smelter, which James named Manchester, after his hometown in England. The settlement grew into a market town supplying the needs of the surrounding area. James married a Spanish born Bolivian, Maria De La Inglesia, and their three children were educated in England. James died in Bolivia, date unknown.

Today only the largest scale maps show Manchester, a small town situated at a crossroads (almost certainly single tracks passable by vehicles with difficulty) deep in Bolivian Amazonia. Main access is by river, the traditional highway for all traffic in the Amazon. The local economy is based around cattle and arable farming.

BOLIVIA
MANCHESTER, (Pando District)

Transport links
Roads   Unmetalled roads (tracks) to nearby villages. A new road is under construction (with Japanese help) linking Riberalta with Trinidad, San Borja and the capital La Paz.
Water   On the River Manuripi. Rivers form the main highways for goods and people.
Air   Nearest airport Cobija (60 miles) – connections to Riberalta (105 miles) - services to La Paz, Santa Cruz, Trinidad and Guayaramerin.
Climate   Hot and humid. Rainy season November to March.
Elevation   603 ft. above sea level.
Local press   n/a
Information provided by Dr. Rene Navarro, Bolivian Embassy, London and Father Bill Murphy.

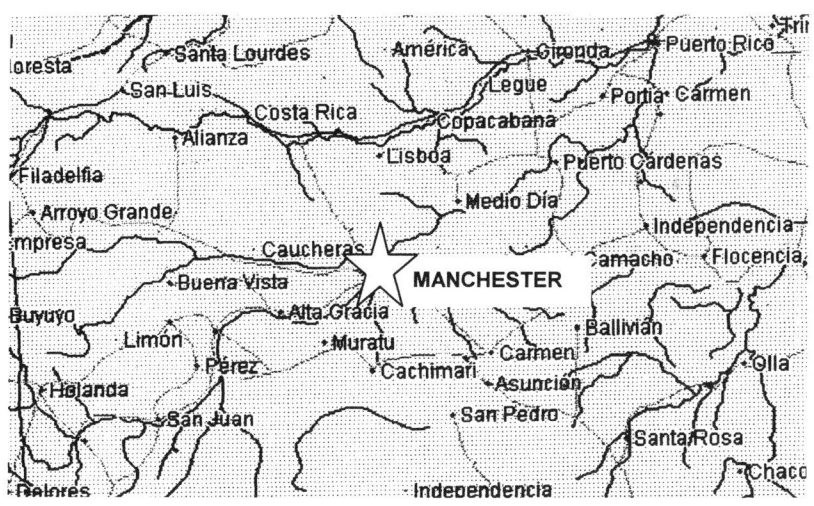

Manchester deep in the Bolivian Amazon – one of many small towns
linked by tributaries of the Amazon River

CANADA

I had expected the same proliferation of Manchesters in Canada as I had found in the United States. This was not to be the case and I had to hunt very hard indeed to turn up just a mere handful. I can offer no explanation as to why Manchesters are so few and far between in Canada and yet so thick on the ground in the United States.

Canada – each "star" a Manchester. Compare
this with the map of the United States on page 26

MANCHESTER,
ONTARIO
(Municipality of Durham)

Location   Latitude 44.04 N. Longitude 78.59 E.
             Province of Ontario, 38 miles north east of Toronto, part of the
             Township of Schugog (Administrative District).
             Port Perry 2 miles.
Population   100 (estimated)
        The first permanent European settler in this part of Canada was Rueben Crandell who arrived in the locality with his wife and young child in 1821. He set to and built a log cabin on a site near the present hamlet of Manchester. He had been born in New York State in 1797 but as a result of the War of 1812 between Britain and the fledgling USA the Crandell family

MANCHESTER, ONTARIO
(Municipality of Durham)

moved to Prince Edward County in Canada, wishing to remain under the British flag. He was but twenty-one years of age when he and his young wife and child travelled along the well-established "Indian Footpath" linking Lake Ontario with Lake Scugog. Crandell and his wife Catherine raised twelve children and became major landowners in the area. He died in 1874 at the age of seventy-seven, a wealthy and widely respected man. Other settlers followed Crandell and gradually a number of small settlements grew up in the area, one of which was named Manchester. The site was originally known as "Fitchett's Corners" after a local settler whose homestead was near a tollgate on the plank road between Prince Albert and Uxbridge.

Little is known of the history of the hamlet but the whole area became the centre of the logging industry. Many of the local people are descendants of the original mainly Scottish, Irish and Dutch settlers. Agriculture remains important in the local economy. Today the hamlet boasts two doughnut shops, a restaurant/coffee shop, a satellite antenna business and a road maintenance depot. The area is a popular recreational centre for both summer and winter visitors. Daniel Palmer, the founder of the modern form of chiropractic healing, was born in nearby Port Perry.

Transport links
Road   At the intersection of Highways 12 and 7A, 15 miles north of
            Highway 401.
Rail   Uxbridge 6 miles.
Air   Toronto International 38 miles.
Climate   Average temperatures - Summer 68F. (20C.), Winter -11F.
            (-6C).
Elevation   918 ft. above sea level.
Local press: Port Perry Star, Ed. Peter Hudson, 188 Main Street,
            Port Perry, LGL1, Tel. 958 8566.
            Schugog Citizen, Ed. John McLelland, 36 Water St.,
            Port Perry. Tel. 985 6397.
Information provided by Karen McLean, Uxbridge Town Library, Ontario and D. Farquharson, Port Perry High School.

MANCHESTER, NOVA SCOTIA
(Guysborough Municipal District)

Location   Latitude 45.27N. Longitude 61.28W.
An unincorporated area within Guysborough comprising of Manchester, Manchester South and Manchester Middle.

MANCHESTER LAKE
(Fort Smith Region)

Location   Latitude 61.28N. Longitude107.29W.
Northwest Territories near Yellowknife.
A check of the trading posts in the Northwest Territories from 1870 to 1970 by the Yellowknife librarian, Eileen Murdoch, revealed no mention of a Manchester. The lake was named Manchester on 13th. March, 1947 after *"a British city that was bombed in World War II"*, presumably at the suggestion of a local citizen with a Manchester connection.
Information provided by Eileen Murdoch, Yellowknife Public Library, Box 694, Yellowknife, Northwest Territories, X1A 2N5 Canada.

MANCHESTER ISLAND
(North West Territories)

One of the numerous small uninhabited islands south of the Taltson River and east of Great Slave Lake. Many were given names by the early trappers before the area was fully explored and mapped. No record exists as to why this particular island was so named.
Information provided by Peter Hudson, 188 Main St., Port Perry, L9 L1.

BLACKLEY HAVEN
(North West Territories)

Location   Latitude 76.01N. Longitude 116.32W
Lying well within the Arctic Circle, Blackley Haven is a bay on one of the Queen Elizabeth Islands.
The early pioneers carried the name of their hometown city of Manchester from pole to pole (well, almost!). In this particular case it was one of the districts of the city that was remembered, perhaps with a touch of homesickness, in the inhospitable Arctic not far from the Magnetic Pole.
Blackley Haven lies in the Innuitian Region, part of the Arctic Archipelago, an area mostly covered in glaciers or polar deserts. Records show that Blackley Haven was named by *"Richards, 1853, possibly after BLACKLEY, a suburb of Manchester, England"* Perhaps it is cheating slightly to include suburbs in this World of Manchesters but I thought Blackley and Didsbury worthy of a passing mention.

DIDSBURY
(Alberta)

Location   Latitude 51.47N. Longitude 114.06W.

Population   3553 (1996)

As with Blackley Haven I came across Didsbury by chance when searching for Canadian Manchesters. Didsbury is a small town, the County Seat of Mountain View County, Alberta, about forty miles north of Calgary, on the route from Calgary to Edmonton. It was first settled by a number of farming families in the 1880's and derived its name from *"the Town of Didsbury in Manchester, England"*. Among the early settlers were the descendants of Dutch Mennonites (a Protestant sect) and one of the first buildings erected was a Mennonite church, soon followed by churches of other religions. The town became the centre of a prosperous farming community. A railway station was opened in 1897 and by 1909 the town had 709 residents. A disastrous fire on New Year's Day in 1914 destroyed much of the business district but the citizens set to and quickly rebuilt the thirty-five properties destroyed by the fire.

Agriculture, oil and gas are the mainstay industries of the town today, which continues to serve most of the needs of the local community. Additional services are readily accessible at nearby Calgary and Red Deer.

Transport links

Road   Ring road system gives direct access to Highways 2 and 2A (Calgary/Edmonton).

Rail   CPR line to Calgary/Edmonton.

Air   Didsbury-Olds Airport (light aircraft); Calgary International Airport 40 miles.

Climate   Continental – cold winters with warm summers.

Elevation 3368 feet above sea level.

Local press n/a

Information via Internet.

JAMAICA
Manchester Parish
(Middlesex County)

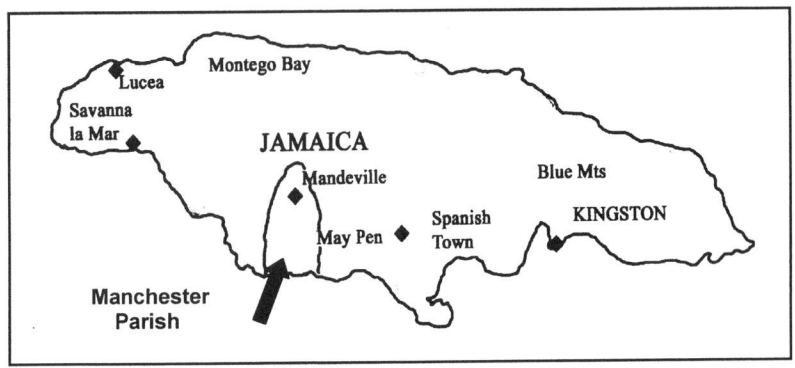

Manchester Parish extends from Trelawny in the north to
the blue waters of the Caribbean in the south.

Location   Latitude 19.90N. Longitude 77.16W.
Population: 164,979 (1991)

A number of Jamaicans, now living happily in the original
Manchester in England, may well have exchanged one Manchester for
another if they emigrated from Manchester Parish. They have brightened up
our lives by bringing a touch of Caribbean sparkle and *joie de vivre* – and a
new cuisine! – to what was a rather dour northern city.

The first European visitor to Jamaica was Christopher Columbus in
1494. He found the gentle Arawak people living contentedly on their "isle of
springs" (Xaymaca). However, Spanish settlement did not begin in earnest
until the early sixteenth century, only for it to be halted when the British
captured the island in 1665. It was to remain under British rule for the next
three hundred years, achieving independence in 1962.

A mountainous area with deeply dissected valleys, Manchester Parish
is approximately 400 square miles in area bounded to the north by Trelawny
and by the Caribbean Sea to the south. The Parish came into being after a
successful petition to the House of Assembly by local citizens of Mile Gully,
May Day and Carpenter's Mountains. They claimed that they were too far
away from the existing administrative and ecclesiastical centres and
requested a new parish be established. This was accepted and an Act passed
in 1814 created the new Parish of Manchester. It was named in honour of the
Duke of Manchester, the Governor of the island. A site for the parish capital
was selected which was to be named Mandeville after the Duke's eldest son.

JAMAICA
(Manchester Parish)

Parish officers were appointed and it was decided to build a courthouse, a church, a parsonage and a jail or workhouse. Law and religion obviously came top in their list of priorities! Contracts for the erection of these buildings were awarded in October 1816 at a cost of £6,800. Mandeville was built along the lines of an English country town with the parish church and Georgian courthouse facing the town green.

The Vestry was both the municipal and ecclesiastical authority of Manchester Parish, its membership being made up of magistrates and elected Vestrymen, together with the Rector and two Churchwardens. To be elected a Vestryman a candidate had to be British and *"be in possession of ten Slaves or the receipt of £120 as salary"*. Eighty-six citizens qualified to stand under these terms in 1819. In the same year a Mr. Richardson was called upon to resign as a Vestryman on the grounds that he was an alien (i.e. not British). The qualifications were raised the following year to twenty slaves or a salary of £200 per year. Thus only the relatively well off would qualify.

Attendance at Vestry meetings was taken very seriously, a fine of £5 being imposed on each absentee when a meeting fell through for lack of a quorum. This was raised to £10 for a second consecutive absence - a very hefty fine in those days. Members were also fined forty shillings if they left a meeting without the permission of the Chairman.

The Vestry Minutes provide a fascinating glimpse into everyday life in Manchester Parish. The Minutes record that in 1820 the Rector was given permission to rent the Rectory as a tavern to Mr. John Hollingworth, as he felt the site of the Rectory was unsuitable for himself and his family. This action led to acrimony and dissent among members of the Vestry, as no doubt it would today!

The 1821 Minutes reveal that several magistrates refused to pay their share of the cost of the dinner to mark the Consecration of the Church and £86.16.2 had to be put aside to pay for the deficiency. It must have been an extraordinarily good dinner for this was a very large sum, as evidenced by the rejection of the Rector's earlier request for £85.16.8 for Prayer Books, *"on account of the enormity of the charge"*. Food for the inner man was obviously considered to be more important than food for the soul!

Another entry in the Minutes refers to the Communion Cup which was considered unsuitable, being too large. After the death of its donor the cup was given as a trophy for a horse race, *"to be run for annually as may be directed"* and a new and more suitable Communion cup was purchased. Think of the outcry today if a Communion Cup was used for this purpose!

JAMAICA
(Manchester Parish)

A population count in 1825 gave the following figures for Manchester Parish:

	Males	Females	Total
White Inhabitants	225	47	272
Free People of Colour	373	406	779
Slaves	8505	8559	17064

The abolition of slavery throughout the British Empire in 1833 brought the building of schools and churches to educate the newly freed slaves and their children. The nineteenth century rural economy has continued relatively unchanged to this day, albeit with more modern methods of farming and distribution. Citrus fruits remain the main crop - oranges, grapefruit, ortaniques (a cross between an orange and a tangerine) and tangerines. Other crops include potatoes, yams and coffee. The bauxite industry is also important and a growing number of tourists are visiting the area.

Norman Washington Manley, the first Prime Minister when the island was granted internal self-government in 1959, was born in Manchester Parish and his birthday is celebrated every 4th July. Many of the early nineteenth century buildings still stand, among them the Mandeville Court House erected in 1817.

Transport links

Road	Road links to all parts of the island.
Water	Many local and inter-island ferry services.
Air	Donald Sangster International Airport, Montego Bay (70 miles); Norman Manley Airport, Kingston (70 miles).
Climate	Tropical with wide variations between mountainous areas. Occasional hurricanes.
Elevation	From sea level to over 3000 ft.
Local press	The Mandeville Weekly, Ed. Percival Clayton, Reliable Printers, 2 Bally Hooly Road, Mandeville. Tel. 809-962-6065.

Information provided by Mrs. K.V.Barton, Regional Librarian, Manchester Parish Library Mandeville, Jamaica.

THE UNITED STATES

The United States of America contains, by my count, over fifty inhabited Manchesters ranging from the city in New Hampshire to tiny hamlets simply recorded as a "populated place" by the Census Bureau. There are also many Manchester Townships to be found, former administrative areas which no longer serve that purpose and most of which now are little more than a name on a map. Manchester also lives on in the names of many schools, churches, historic post offices, lakes and reservoirs, mountains and even abandoned gold and silver mines.

I have given, where known, the reason for the choice of Manchester as a name for the town. Most come from a connection of the early settlers with hometown Manchester, others in admiration, hoping that the new settlement will eventually emulate the original great city in England. Where the origin of the name has been lost in the mists of time, through lack of written records or whatever, it is reasonable to assume that similar reasons prevailed when the time came to give a new settlement a name. Population figures in the main are taken from the year 2000 Census although, in one or two cases, these figures are not yet available and the 1990 Census figures have been used.

It is now a cliché to talk about "small town America" but that is exactly what many of the Manchesters are; small towns first settled because of the local natural resources, timber especially and, in one case, a plentiful supply of salt. Crossroads were an ideal position to found a new settlement to serve the needs of travellers but it was the coming of the railroads that really led to the western expansion of settlements. Many small settlements were created to serve the needs of the railroad. Those that existed before the railroads came boomed if the railroad served the town or declined, often to the point of extinction, if the railroad passed them by. No wonder that many settlements offered large bribes to the railroad companies to run the track through the town!

Some small towns flourished for a time, Manchesters among them, and then declined as economic condition turned against them or "progress", often in the form of new highways, passed them by. Those that have survived have largely changed in character, often becoming dormitory towns for commuters or taking to tourism where the locality has attractions for visitors. So, in alphabetical order, let us begin our journey through the Manchesters of the United States.

THE UNITED STATES

The distribution of Manchesters in the United States
Note the concentration in the eastern and central states

MANCHESTER, ALABAMA
(Walker County)

Location   Latitude 33.54N. Longitude 87.18W.
Northwest Alabama, north of US Federal Highway 78. Six miles north of Jasper.

Population   Below 100

As with so many other settlements in America this village of Manchester owes its foundation to the coming of the railroad. Its short life began early in this century after the purchase of vast timber holdings in the area by the Western Electric Company. In 1906 a new railroad, the Alabama Central, was constructed to run from Jasper to a logging centre that quickly grew into the village that was later to be called Manchester. There is no record of why the name Manchester was chosen.

The village comprised of the main logging pond, the commissary (stores) and houses for the workers and their families. Amongst the families attracted to the village by the work available were the Russells, Camps, Brittons, Mattinglys, Hubbards, Covingtons, Atwoods, Less' Sallades' J.Metzger, a Captain White and others.

MANCHESTER, ALABAMA
(Walker County)

By 1910 Manchester was a thriving community and so it remained until 1926 when the local timber supply was exhausted. The logging plant closed and, as no other work was available in the locality, the inhabitants moved on to seek work elsewhere. Today Manchester, Alabama is just a semi-deserted village on a bend in the Blackwater Creek. All local services for the small number of people who remain in the Manchester area are administered from Jasper.

Transport links

Road	On State Highway 195 and 4 miles north of US Federal 78.
Rail	Jasper (6 miles).
Water	Blackwater River (12 miles), navigable channel depth 9 ft.
Air	Bevill Field (10 miles). Nearest commercial airfield Birmingham (50 miles).
Climate	Short moderate winters, long warm summers. Mean temperatures Winter 50F, Summer 80F. Annual rainfall 54 inches
Elevation	470 feet above sea level.
Local press	Daily Mountain Eagle (Jasper). Birmingham News-Post Herald, 2200 North Avenue, B'ham.
Zip Code(s)	35501.
Reference	"History of Alabama" – Owen.

Also in Walker County - Manchester Division, an administrative sub-division of Walker County including Manchester Village, Manchester School, Manchester Post Office (historical) and Manchester Mine.

Information provided by Walker County Chamber of Commerce, Jasper and by the United States Government Information Service (USGIS) via Internet

MANCHESTER, ALABAMA
(Marshall County)

Location	Latitude 34.24N. Longitude 86.20W. At the junction of Tennessee River/Guntersville Lake. Guntersville (5 miles).
Population	Not recorded. Too small to be marked on maps and although listed as a "populated place " by the US Census Bureau, no population figure is given, indicating a very small hamlet or homestead.

Transport links

Road	Dirt road off State Highway 69.
River	Tennessee River (navigable).

MANCHESTER, ALABAMA
(Marshall County)

Rail   CSX Railroad.
Air   Guntersville Airport (5 miles); Huntsville/Madison County Jetplex (45 minutes by road); Birmingham International Airport (90 minutes by road).
Climate   Short moderate winters with long warm summers. Marshall County is one of the colder parts of the State with an annual average temperature of about 60F.
Elevation   600 feet above sea level.
Local press   The Gadsden Times, PO Box 188, 401 Locust St., Gadsden, AL. Zip Code(s) 35976 (Guntersville)
Information provided by the United States Government Information Service (USGIS) via Internet.

MANCHESTER, ARKANSAS
(Dallas County)

Location   Latitude 34.02N. Longitude 92.86W.
                At the intersection of Highways 7 & 8 in south central Arkansas, approximately 60 miles south of Little Rock. Southeast of Pine Bluff - near Sparkman, Pine Grove, and Holly Springs.
Population   380
        Manchester Township lies in Dallas County (established 1845), an area of gently rolling timberlands. This part of south central Arkansas was originally the home of the Caddo tribe of Native Americans who were driven from their homelands in the clearances of the 1840's. This led to a large influx of European settlers mainly from the southern states. Their knowledge of cotton cultivation soon resulted in many large plantations being established. In addition small settlements like Manchester came into being to take advantage of the abundant timber resources.
        Manchester Township is now an historic administrative unit covering the local area as a sub-division of the county. The original settlement is too small to be shown on any but the most detailed of maps.
Transport links
Road   Near the intersection of State Highways 8 & 9, north of Sparkman.
Air   Nearest airport, Little Rock (65 miles).
Climate   Moderately long, hot summers; short, mild winters. Abundant rainfall.

28

MANCHESTER, ARKANSAS
(Dallas County)

Elevation   382 – 584 ft. above sea level.
Local press   The Morning News.
Zip   71725
Also in Arkansas - Manchester Cemetery (Mississippi County), Manchester Church and the historic former Manchester Township administrative area (Clark County).
References   Dallas County History via Internet.
Information provided by the United States Government Information Service (USGIS) via Internet.

MANCHESTER, CALIFORNIA
(Mendocino County)

Location   Latitude 38.58N. Longitude 123.41W.
               On the Pacific Coast Highway 38 miles south of Fort Bragg, 6 miles north of Point Arena.
Population   462 (excluding summer visitors)
   The European "discovery" of California in 1542 is officially credited to the Spaniard Juan Rodriguez Cabrillo, although another Spanish explorer, Hernando Cortez, had sailed north from Mexico seven years earlier and given the name California to that part of the coast. Francis Drake visited the area in 1579 renaming it Nova (New) Albion, partly because the white cliffs were reminiscent of the white cliffs of Dover and claiming it for Elizabeth 1. Drake's Bay, along the coast from Manchester Beach, is so named to commemorate his visit.

"California Dreaming" – Manchester (and Manchester Beach)
north of San Francisco

MANCHESTER, CALIFORNIA
(Mendocino County)

It was in this bay, in 1559, that Drake careened his ship the "Golden Hind" to prepare her for the long voyage back to England loaded down with all the Spanish treasure he had captured. This landing, according to Master Francis Fletcher, was made at latitude 38.30N. which is just south of present day Manchester Beach.

There was some excitement recently caused by the discovery of the remains of what is believed to be a fort constructed by Sir Francis Drake's men. If this is proved to be the case it will indicate that Drake's visit to California was of a much longer duration than previously believed. Before leaving Drake ordered a stout post to be erected bearing a brass plate recording his visit and claiming the land for Queen Elizabeth. No trace of this post or plate has been found.

Europeans first settled the Manchester area in the latter part of the 19th Century and found that the rich fertile soil and the warm, relatively fog free climate, made the area ideal for arable and dairy farming. Manchester is a small town approximately 150 miles north of San Francisco, being identified by a post office and a single general store. This is the heartland of Mendocino County dairy country and many of the local people are direct descendants of the original pioneer settlers. Those who are not retired work mainly on the ranches or logging. The stretch of coastline from the Garcia River to Alder Creek is known as Manchester Beach. The coast is famous for the flocks of white Whistling Swans, a protected species, which overwinter by the Garcia River.

Manchester State Beach is popular with tourists and there are a number of campsites among the meadows and sand dunes. Stretching for well over five miles the beach offers exceptional fishing, whale watching (November to March) and beachcombing. It is the landfall for several trans-Pacific undersea telephone cables including the latest 5300-mile fibre optic cable linking the U.S.A. and Japan.

The beautiful Tundra Swans (the Whistling Swans)
overwinter just south of Manchester Beach

30

MANCHESTER, CALIFORNIA
(Mendocino County)

Point Arena Lighthouse near Manchester Beach

Transport links
Air   San Francisco International Airport.
Road   State Highway 1 – a scenic highway along the Pacific coast to San Francisco.
Climate   Dry summers, mild winters. Annual rainfall 20 inches (51 cm.) mainly December to February.
Elevation   110 feet above sea level rising to 4500 feet.
Local press Mendocino Beacon, 45066 Ukiah St., Mendocino, CA 95460.
Zip   95459
Also in California - Mount Manchester (3600 ft.) San Bernardino County, (Lat. 35.01N, Long. 114.43W). There are Manchester Elementary Schools in Mendocino County, Fresno and Los Angeles and a Manchester Shopping Centre in Fresno.
Information provided by Beverly Easterday, Willits Chamber of Commerce.

COLORADO

Although no inhabited places retain the name of Manchester in the State of Colorado, the name lives on in the former gold mining area around Colorado Springs. There is a Manchester Lake (reservoir) in Gilpin County, Manchester Creek (Teller County), and several inactive gold and silver mines named Manchester in Boulder and Gilpin Counties.

MANCHESTER, CONNECTICUT
(Hartford County)
"The City of Village Charm"

Location   Latitude 41.77 N. Longitude 72.52 W.
                On the Hockanum River in central Connecticut, five miles due
                west of Hartford, the state capital.
Population   54,740 (Central Manchester 30,595)

Connecticut, the southernmost of the New England states, is one of the original thirteen colonies that formed the United States. The central lowland area of the fertile Connecticut River valley, including the site of present-day Manchester, was originally the territory of the Pequot Native Americans. In 1633 a group of Dutch settlers journeyed from the colony of New Netherlands to found the first European settlement. A few years later the Rev. Thomas Hooker led a group of about one hundred English settlers from Massachusetts into the area. In 1672 a parcel of land known as the Five Mile Tract was purchased from the Mohegan Indians (who had driven out the Pequot) to found a new settlement. This early settlement grew into the town of Hartford as records of the time reveal: -

"At a Town Metting of the Inhabitants of ye Town of Hartford held ffebr 13th 1706/7 It was Voated and agreed that a Committy be Chosen To defend the Rights of the Town on the East Side of the great River, but Especially their Right in all or any part of the fiue Miles."

Present day Manchester was originally known as Orford Parish, part of the town of Hartford mentioned above. The Parish later became known as East Hartford until 1823 when it was separately incorporated as the town of Manchester. Although it has been claimed that the name came from Manchester, England, from where there was much early migration, this has been disputed. Nevertheless, as textiles were produced in the area from the late 18th century onwards it is not unreasonable to assume that this may have influenced the choice of the name Manchester for the new township.

The introduction of the manufacture of silk by the Cheney Brothers in 1839, together with the opening of the Pitkin Glass Works and a number of cotton mills, transformed Manchester from a rural township into a thriving industrial centre. The silk mills remained the town's most important

MANCHESTER, CONNECTICUT
(Hartford County)

The Town Crest
(Courtesy of the Town of Manchester, Connecticut)

industrial activity throughout the nineteenth and early twentieth centuries and the Cheney influence extended to all aspects of community life - utilities, health, education, welfare, etc. Interestingly, in the nineteenth century, the town was also famous for the manufacture of grandfather clocks.

The Second World War saw the introduction of many new industries which resulted in a dramatic rise in the population from twenty three thousand in 1940 to thirty five thousand by 1950. Present day manufacturing industry includes car parts, soap, paper products and textiles. Today Manchester includes the industrial South Manchester Village and the residential area of Manchester Green that together make a fair sized town of over fifty thousand people.

Transport links
Road   On the US Interstate 84.
Air   Bradley International Airport 10 miles.
Climate   Cold winters, warm summers. Annual rainfall 42 inches.
Elevation   177 feet above sea level.
Local press The Hartford Courant.
Zip(s)   06040, 06043.
Reference   "Connecticut Town Origins" - Helen Earle Sellars (Pequot Press).
            Mary Cheney Library Annual Report 1994. (Mary Cheney Library).
Also within Hartford County - Manchester Town (administrative area), Manchester Green & Manchester Country Club.
Information provided by the Librarian, Mary Cheney Library, Hartford; Richard Sartor, General Manager, Town of Manchester; Darcy Arcand,

MANCHESTER, CONNECTICUT
(Hartford County)

Director, Citizens Services and Information, Town of Manchester and John Anderson, Greater Manchester Chamber of Commerce.

Manchester, Hartford County, Connecticut
Circa 1940
(Photo courtesy of the Town of Manchester)

MANCHESTER, GEORGIA
(Meriwether County)
"The Magic City"

Location   Latitude 32.51N. Longitude 84.37W.
West central Georgia, in the foothills of the Appalachian Mountains. On State Highway 41, sixty miles south of Atlanta (State Capital), forty miles north east of Columbus.

Population   6125 (Greater Manchester area); City of Manchester 3988

After the War of Independence the region remained Native American territory until 1825 when the Treaty of Indian Springs ceded it to the United States. After the signing of the Treaty settlers flooded into the area in which the town of Manchester was later to be founded. The new homesteads were mainly scattered along the slopes of Pine Mountain where the water was pure and the air free from malaria, the scourge of pioneer settlers.

The coming of the railroads in the later nineteenth century opened up more of the territory and Manchester was one of the many small towns which came into being as a result. The town was established in 1907 as a consequence of being chosen as the site for the junction of three main lines of the Atlanta, Birmingham and Atlantic railroad, the 'ABA'. At the same time, Callaway Cotton Mills opened a new mill and the owner, Fuller E.Callaway, sold building plots for $75 each to prospective residents.

MANCHESTER, GEORGIA
(Meriwether County)

The town was laid out in 1908 and chartered on the 16th August 1909, being named after Manchester, England, possibly because of the cotton connection. The town developed very quickly and by 1912 Manchester had become the largest town in Meriwether County and its surrounding area. Building continued apace; houses, shops, schools and churches and proper water and sewage systems were installed, streets being named after persons and trees. Other industry was attracted and the railroad workshops extended. Much of the development of the town came about through the activities of the mill owners who provided houses, a church, school and recreation centre for the mill operatives. The Callaway Foundation has continued to provide facilities for the townsfolk.

In 1924 Franklin Delano Roosevelt, 32nd President of the United States (1933-45), made his second home in nearby town of Warm Springs. As a sufferer from polio he was attracted by the mineral springs which he found gave great relief. The house he had built there became known as "The Little White House" and is a popular place for tourists to visit.

Today the modern town of Manchester, "The Magic City" as it likes to be styled, is undergoing something of a regeneration. The population is up nearly 10% since 1990 and much of the town has been improved by refurbishment. A new 250-acre industrial park has been built and white crepe myrtle trees have been planted along all of Main Street. The largest industrial employer is Goody Products Inc. (hair & personal care items). Other main employers are the service industries, wood products, small-scale manufacturing, and wholesale and retail trades. Approximately 47% of the labour force commutes to work outside the town.

Transport links

Road   On State Highway 41.

Rail   Norfolk Southern and CSX rail services (local).

Air   Nearest commercial air service Columbus (35 miles). Nearest public airport Warm Springs (4 miles).

Water   Nearest navigable river - Chattahoochee (9ft.channel depth)

Climate   Winters generally mild, summers warm and humid. Average annual temperature 63F. Annual rainfall 44 inches.

Elevation 883 feet above sea level.

Local press Manchester Star Mercury, (weekly), Editor Bob Tribble, PO Box 426, Manchester, GA 31816.
Manchester Free Press, Editor Henry Barnes, PO Box 925, Greenville, 31816; Columbus Ledger Enquirer (daily).

Zip   31816

MANCHESTER, GEORGIA
(Meriwether County)

Reference   "Historical Account of Meriwether County, 1827-1974"
compiled by Roger P.Pinkston and from the Manchester,
Georgia Home Page via Internet.
Information provided by Natalie Maddocks, Meriwether County Chamber of
Commerce; Jennifer Elliot, Manchester Development Authority;
Larry R. Rains; Jaynie Nesmith, Meriwether County Chamber of Commerce
and Donna Wesley, Town of Manchester.

Any excuse for a Parade! Main Street Paving Celebration
Manchester, Georgia (date unknown)
(Photo courtesy of Manchester Development Authority)

MANCHESTER, GEORGIA
(Meriwether County)

"Magic Hill" in Manchester, Georgia where cars (and bikes) appear to freewheel uphill! Sadly, since this picture was taken, the hill has been levelled so the "magic" is no more.
(Photo courtesy of Larry R. Rains)

Arial view of Manchester, Georgia
(Photo courtesy of the Manchester Development Authority)

MANCHESTER, GEORGIA
(Meriwether County)

The Fire Department in Georgia are trained to
tackle anything - except perhaps a spelling test!
(Photo courtesy of the Manchester Development Authority)

MANCHESTER, ILLINOIS
(Scott County)

Location   Latitude 39.32N. Longitude 90.19W.
A small country town in east central Illinois. Approximately
15 miles south east of Jacksonville and 40 miles south east of
Springfield.

Population   354 (Manchester Village); 664 (Manchester Precinct)
Manchester lies in the plains area of Illinois, a rich farming area
where "the land is level as far as the eye can see". In 1819 the Kickapoo
Indians ceded to the United States a tract of land that included territory, now
known as Scott County, in which Manchester is situated. In return for less
than one-sixth of a cent per acre and the promise of a permanent home
beyond the Mississippi, the Kickapoo gave up a vast area including the great
prairie lands of central Illinois.

It was in this area, in the same year, that a small group of Europeans
came across a spring, with a burned out settlement nearby, where prairie hay
had been harvested the previous year. This site, which became known as
Burnt Hay Stacks Spring, is where Manchester now stands. Early records
indicate "the spot where Manchester now stands was first settled in 1821 by
Mr Marks." He was a farmer who, apart from owning the land, kept a tavern
in Manchester in the early days. His remains still lie in the village cemetery.

38

MANCHESTER, ILLINOIS
(Scott County)

The town site was platted (surveyed and divided into lots) in 1831. The name Manchester was adopted in 1832, after Manchester, England, because many of the settlers came from that city. In 1839 Morgan County was sub-divided and Scott County, which included Manchester, came into being. As more settlers came the village gradually expanded though the economy was still based on agriculture and timber. However, the Civil War saw a development of small-scale manufacturing, wagon making and farm implements. The early settlers also brought their own forms of religion and soon the town had Baptist, Methodist and Presbyterian churches.

The town of Manchester was incorporated in April 1861, the Act stating that the town boundaries were to be one square mile. A Town Council was elected consisting of a President and four Trustees. After the end of the Civil War small-scale manufacturing declined and Manchester reverted to being a centre for the local farming community. The town was fortunate in being a stagecoach stop which served to keep the residents in touch with the outside world. The stagecoach in turn gave way to the Chicago & Alton Railroad which gave direct access to St. Louis and Chicago. The railroad was used to transport farm produce and pigs to East St. Louis.

In 1907 the first telephone was installed - a party line shared by ten subscribers! Improved communications have resulted in economic development bypassing many small towns like Manchester, leaving life to continue largely undisturbed by progress. The town today still retains a school, two churches and several stores catering for the needs of local residents who are mostly engaged in agriculture.

Transport links

Road	On Highway 267, adjacent to US Federal 67.
Air	Jacksonville (15 miles) and Springfield (40 miles) airports for commercial air services.
Climate	Continental climate - warm summers, cold winters. Average annual temperature 53F (11.7C).
Elevation	690 feet above sea level.
Local press	The State Journal Register, One Copley Plaza, Springfield, IL. 62701.
Zip	62663

Information provided by Mary Ellen Jameson.

A WORLD OF MANCHESTERS

MANCHESTER, ILLINOIS
(Boone County)

Location   Latitude 42.45N. Longitude 88.88W.
North central Illinois, near the border with Wisconsin.
15 miles north east of Rockford
Population 931

In the early years of the nineteenth century the rolling prairies of central Illinois, ideal farming country, proved to be the magnet that first attracted settlers from New York and New England. Boone County was formed in 1836, taking its name from the famous frontier pioneer Daniel Boone. Although Manchester formed one of the eight townships of the county, it would appear that the town itself has faded away with the passage of time. Only the name Manchester Township survives as a county sub division that formerly had administrative responsibilities for the local area.

Two buildings retain the link, at least in name, with the past. Manchester School and Manchester Church both continue to serve the needs of the local community.

Transport links
Road   On Highway 267 (St. Louis/Jacksonville)
Air   Rockford 15 miles, Chicago International Airport 54 miles.
Climate   Continental climate with warm summers and cold winters.
Average temperatures – July 82F. January 15F.
Average annual rainfall 32 inches.
Local press   Rockford Register Star, 99 East State Street, Rockford, IL. 61104.
Zip(s)   61011, 61073, 61080
Reference   "The Historical Encyclopedia of Illinois" via Internet.

MANCHESTER, INDIANA
(Dearborn County)

Location   Latitude 39.10N. Longitude 85.00W.
Very small village on Highway 48, near Lawrenceburg.
Cincinnati (Ohio) 20 miles due east.
Population   Below 100 (Manchester Village);
2930 (Manchester Township)

In the late eighteenth and early nineteenth centuries the site of what was to become Manchester was just a convenient overnight stopping place for cattle being driven to the shipping point on the Ohio River about twelve miles distant, a one day's cattle drive. It was also a resting point for travellers using the primitive turnpikes serving the pioneer settlements.

The first land sale on the Manchester site was to David Blane in 1809

MANCHESTER, INDIANA
(Dearborn County)

but the first permanent settlement came in 1815 when the two McCracken brothers, Mark and Robert accompanied by their mother, built a cabin in the neighbourhood. It was an isolated spot and therefore Robert cut a seven-mile wagon road through virgin territory to the nearest settlement at Cambridge - a truly remarkable feat that exemplified the spirit and determination of the early pioneers.

The McCracken's nearest neighbours were four to five miles away towards the Ohio River, the land to the west being *"an unbroken and interminable wilderness"*. Another early settler, Judge Cotton from Maine, who settled in Manchester in 1818, described returning home at night to his cabin along a footpath he had "blazed" as a shortcut to the settlement. He wrote, *"Many is the time and oft, that I have entered this dismal and solitary homeward path, when for a good part of the way, it was so dark that I could not see my hand to save me - was compelled to feel out the path with my feet, with my heart in my mouth, my hair well nigh erect, and my blood nearly curdled, for the prowling wolves were about my path and had often raised their hideous yells in my very door yard"*.

The end of the war against Britain in 1815, which also lessened the danger from Native American tribes supporting the British, led to what was known as the "Ohio Fever". The prospect of land in abundance caused families from the Eastern states to rush to settle in the heartland states of America. One large group of fifteen pioneering families, seventy-eight souls in total with ten wagons and twenty-four horses, aroused great public interest and were spoken of by newspapers of the time as "the land fleet". Their journey took them overland via Portland, Albany to the Allegheny River then by boat and raft to Pittsburgh and down the Ohio River on flat-bottomed boats to their final landing place at Lawrenceburg - overall an epic journey even in those pioneering days. From there most of them settled on the Indiana side of the great Ohio River on what was then known as Green Brier Ridge, later to become Manchester.

The first settlers found the site of Manchester a thickly wooded area with some of the largest and tallest trees east of California, which provided a plentiful supply of timber for houses and barns. Later the Jaquith family developed a thriving family cooperage business turning the great oaks into pork barrels. Early Manchester spread along a four-mile stretch of the Lawrenceburg to Napoleon turnpike and comprised of a cluster of four small hamlets, Upper Manchester (Muletown), Middle Manchester, Lower Manchester (Plummertown) and Wright's Corner. Upper Manchester was the most prosperous and boasted a way stop, the Drovers' Inn (still standing), with overnight accommodation for travellers and cattle!

MANCHESTER, INDIANA
(Dearborn County)

Muletown was allegedly named after a mule with a contrary temperament owned by Daniel Northrop, a local inhabitant. Plummertown was named after the Plummer family who settled in the neighbourhood and Wright's Corner related to a prominent local citizen, Charles W. Wright.

The following telling description of life in the early township was written in 1876 by George W. Lane and published in the Aurora Independent, a local newspaper: -

"Soon after the war (The American Civil War) one of the most important settlements of number and character was made in Manchester Township. They suffered many hardships and indeed many deprivations, but they stood their ground like Christian martyrs, and many lived to see tall oaks utilized for other purposes and removed to make room for houses, barns and meadows, and in less than a decade the ridge for miles was under a high state of cultivation, and in the fall, rows of teams would be seen on the road hauling off the surplus of their farms and cooper shops."

An assortment of trades and shops developed in the town to serve the various needs of the turnpike travellers and settlers including a general store, blacksmiths, post office, wagon maker, boots and shoes maker, tannery, a cooper's shop and a doctor. Schools, churches and a Masonic Lodge were erected and in due course a number of flour, grist, saw and carding mills began operating. The mills were powered at various times by various means - water, horse and steam. At a horse mill operated by James Baggs those wishing to use the mill had to provide not only their own horse power but also hand over one eighth of the grist milled in payment!

Over the years many residents rose to prominence and high office at local, county and state level; too many to do full justice to in this brief account. However mention must be made of one of the founding fathers of Manchester, Mark McCracken, a well-known man in his day. As an officer of the county he practised the greatest parsimony with public funds, his motto being that he had a right to be liberal or even extravagant with his own, but never with the people's money. Would that present day politicians took this to heart!

There is no record as to why and when Green Brier Ridge became known as Manchester, the township was never incorporated and today the name remains only as that of an administrative area. What little of the actual town that survives is much as it has always been, a small rural community, a general store, the "Manchester Market" and a restaurant that opens during the summer months. The Market features a "liar's bench" on the porch especially for those civilised folk who like to put the world to rights in conversation and the telling of tall tales.

MANCHESTER, INDIANA
(Dearborn County)

Progress in the form of building development threatens the tranquillity of Manchester, much to the dismay of many residents. The old turnpike has turned into the busy State Highway 48 and the world and his wife pass Manchester by without a second glance.

Transport links

Road On State Highway 48.

Air Cincinnati International 20 miles.

Climate Spring and autumn mid 40's F to mid 60's F. Hot summers, 86 F with high humidity. Cold winters, average temperature ranges 42 F to 26 F.

Elevation 880 feet above sea level.

Local press Dearborn County Register, PO Box 328, 126 W. High St., Lawrenceburg, IN. 47025 Tel. (812) 537 0063. Fax. (812) 537 5576.

Zip(s) 47001, 47002, 47025

Reference "History of Dearborn and Ohio Counties, Indiana" F.E.Weakley & Co., Publishers, Chicago, 1885.
"Dearborn County: A Pictorial History" Vol.1. The Dearborn County Historical Society.
"History of Dearborn County, Indiana" (Her People, Industries and Institutions). Editor Archibald Shaw, B.F.Bowen & Co. Inc., Indianapolis, Indiana, 1915.

Information provided by Clara M. Lewis, via Internet

MANCHESTER, INDIANA
(Montgomery County)

Location Latitude 40.05N. Longitude 86.54W.
North of Crawfordsville

Population Indicated as a populated place by the US Government Geographical Survey but without a population figure. This usually means a population of fewer than 100. No further information available.

Transport links

Road At the junction of Highway 231 and County Road 400N just north of Interstate Highway 74.

Rail Rail link to Lafayette (north) and Crawfordsville (south).

Climate Average temperatures January 25F. July 75F.
Annual rainfall 43.6 inches. Annual snowfall 23.1 inches.

Elevation 757 feet above sea level.

MANCHESTER, INDIANA
(Montgomery County)

Local press Journal Review, Crawfordsville, 110 East Market St., Crawfordsville, IN.47933
Information via Internet

NORTH MANCHESTER, INDIANA
(Wabash County)

Latitude   41.00N. Longitude 85.07W.
East of State Highway 13, south west of Fort Wayne.
Population   6260

This part of Indiana was originally the hunting grounds of the Miami and Potawatomi tribes of Native Americans (an Indian village stood just north of the present site of the Manchester College football field). The Indian Treaties of 1812, 1826 and 1827 opened the area to European settlers and the first house on the site of present day North Manchester was constructed in 1834 when Peter Organ built his log cabin. Organ bought land for $1.25 an acre in the area and laid out plans for a village with 100' wide streets and large $50 housing lots, which remain a feature of the town to this day, though not at the original price! Soon other settlers arrived and the town of Manchester came into being. The town's name was changed to North Manchester in 1839 to avoid confusion with other Manchesters in the Union.

By 1861 the town had grown to about 400 inhabitants, all solidly loyal to the Union throughout the Civil War. Indeed, long before the war broke out, many townspeople had been active in the "underground railroad", the secret network that transported slaves to freedom in false-bottomed wagons. One of the "stations" (resting and hiding places) on the underground freedom railway was at Maurice Place's in North Manchester. Town development stopped during the war as the men went off to fight but resumed after peace came in 1864. Flour and saw mills operated along the Eel River and in 1871 a brickworks was opened which provided bricks for many of the houses still standing today.

However, as was often the case, the town growth really began when the railway arrived; the Cincinnati, Wabash & Michigan - the "Big Four" line opened in 1871.The town missed out on a direct rail connection with Chicago and New York through refusing to pay a $30,000 "bonus" to the Erie railroad to route track through the town. The company promptly by-passed the town three miles to the south! Today rail traffic is restricted to freight only. By the end of the century North Manchester was well established with schools, churches and a Town Board.

NORTH MANCHESTER, INDIANA
(Wabash County)

The new century brought new industries to the town including furniture making, foundry work and even an automobile plant. This was opened in 1908 by D.L. De Witt and produced the first De Witt car in 1909. Production was aimed at four cars per day but before that could be achieved a fire destroyed the factory. Only a very few De Witts are still in existence although an exact replica is on display in the town.

The most famous inhabitant was Thomas R. Marshall, born in North Manchester in 1854, who was Vice-President of the United States for two terms from 1912 under President Woodrow Wilson.

North Manchester has remained a typical small American town, a pleasant place to live with a mix of small businesses, industry and agriculture. The town has attracted many retired people who appreciate the climate, the countryside and the quality of life in the area. There is a thriving community life and excellent sports, educational and cultural facilities. An additional attraction is the old covered bridge, built in 1872 and still in daily use, one of the few left in the county. The town is a popular place for visitors with many shops and restaurants to cater for their needs.

Transport links

Road   Off State Highway 13, fifteen miles south of US Federal 30 and twelve miles north of US Federal 24.
Rail   On Cincinnati, Wabash and Michigan line (freight only).
Air   Nearest airport (local services) Wabash, 15 miles. Indianapolis International 100 miles south.
Climate   Humid continental climate modified by influence of Lake Michigan. Average temperatures Summer 73F. Winter 25F. Average rainfall 36". Average snowfall 40". Winter can be bitter with icy rain and snowstorms.
Elevation   771 feet above sea level.
Local press North Manchester News Journal.
Zip(s)   46962
References "Wabash County History" Bicentennial Edition 1976.
Information provided by Davonne Rogers, Director, North Manchester Public Library.

MANCHESTER, IOWA
(Delaware County)

Location   Latitude 42.29N. Longitude 91.27W.
             The County Seat of Delaware County in east central Iowa. On
             Highway 20 midway between Dubuque (45 miles) and
             Waterloo (45 miles) and Cedar Rapids (45 miles).
Population   5257

The area known as Delaware County was acquired in 1803 by the United States of America from France as part of the Louisiana Purchase. The land was home to the Sac and Fox tribes of Native Americans who ceded part to the United States in 1832, the so called "Blackhawk Purchase" which consisted of a strip of land fifty miles wide along the west bank of the Mississippi River.

The area around the present site of Manchester was prairie land with a few scattered trees when Robert Hutson built the first homestead in 1836. The Manchester site proper was settled a few years later, the village becoming known as Burrington in 1855 after another early settler. It was renamed Manchester in 1858 to avoid confusion with Burlington, Iowa. The choice of the name Manchester is believed to have come from a corruption of the name William Chesterman, a partner of the town's founder, with perhaps some suggestion of a connection with Manchester, England. The town was incorporated in 1866 and is laid out in the typical grid pattern of towns in America.

The real making of the town came with the coming of the railroad. A payment by the townspeople of $13000 to the Dubuque and Pacific Railroad for "additional construction costs", the kind that never appear in the account books, ensured that the line reached Manchester in 1859. This, and the civil war agricultural boom, led to the rapid growth of the town which became the County Seat in 1880. The Delaware County Courthouse, erected in Manchester in 1896 to replace the old log cabin courthouse, is listed on the National Register of Historic Places.

The town has grown around a bend in the Maquoketa River and parks and commercial enterprises line the riverbank. As the County Seat Manchester provides administrative, retail, wholesale, manufacturing and leisure facilities for the surrounding highly productive agricultural area. The main agricultural product is pork, Delaware being the second largest pork-producing county in Iowa. Beef, dairy products, corn & soya beans are also important. Principal manufacturing companies in Manchester include Exide Battery (lead acid batteries), Rockwell International (electronic assembly), Henderson Mfg. (truck equipment) and Tredegar Industries (polyethylene film). The town has an elected Mayor and Council with a paid City Manager.

MANCHESTER, IOWA
(Delaware County)

Transport Links

Road	Highways 13 and 20; thirty miles from Interstate 380.
Rail	Chicago Central & Pacific Railroad.
Water	45 minutes by road from navigable Mississippi River.
Air	Manchester Airport. (45 minutes by road to Cedar Rapids airport).
Climate	Average temperatures Summer 70.4F, Winter 19F. Annual rainfall 33.7 inches. Annual snowfall 35.1 inches.
Elevation	919 ft. above sea level.
Local press	Manchester Press (weekly), Editor Larry Woellert, 109 E.Delaware, Manchester, 1A. Tel. (319) 927 2020.
Zip	52057

Also in Iowa - Manchester, a locality near Marquette (Allamakee County).
Information provided by Flora A Schmidt, Executive Director, Manchester Chamber of Commerce.

MANCHESTER, KANSAS
(Dickinson County)

Location	Latitude 39.05N. Longitude 97.19W. North-west/central Kansas. Off US State 70, 12 miles north of Abilene, 23 miles north east of Selina.
Population	102

The area was first settled by English and Scottish families in the late 1860's and early 1870's, many being Civil War veterans. An English settler by the name of John Trott suggested the name Manchester for the new village as the city in England had much impressed him when his family had passed through en route to Canada. A schoolhouse, built in 1877, was widely known as the Mustard schoolhouse after the first teacher, Miss Maggie Mustard.

The village began to flourish and soon boasted two general stores, two hardware and implement stores, a tin shop, a livery barn, two meat markets, two hotels and a restaurant. There were also three blacksmiths, a barber and a water well driller. A railroad across the County was proposed and the Manchester Town Company was formed in the mid 1880's to facilitate a rail link to the town. The efforts of the company were successful and the Kansas and Western Railroad built and operated a line linking Manchester with Strong City and Superior, Nebraska. A rail link to Barnard was also opened in 1888. Four trains came through each day on the Strong City-Superior route and two trains daily on the Barnard track. A natural depression

47

MANCHESTER, KANSAS
(Dickinson County)

northwest of the town was turned into a reservoir to supply water for the railroad engines. This became known as Manchester Lake and which served the additional purpose of also supplying ice to the community and its two hotels. Mexican labour had been recruited to work on the railroads and some of these migrant workers later settled in Manchester in a "depot city" near the rail link.

The town continued to thrive through to the 1920's with its own local newspaper, the "Manchester Motor" (prior to 1910 the "Sun" and the "News") and its own bank. There were Saturday night band concerts in the gazebo in the main street and the future seemed assured. However, the depression of the 1930's took a heavy toll with many businesses, the bank and the newspaper being forced to close. By 1937 high school classes ended and although the elementary school lingered on a few more years it too closed in 1966. On the retirement of the postmistress the post office closed and gradually the town declined to its present population of around one hundred people, varying little from year to year. Descendants of the early settlers still live in and around Manchester. The weather in this part of Kansas can perhaps best be described as "interesting".

Transport links

Road   Off US Interstate 70 (12 miles).
Rail   On Strong City-Superior branch line.
Air   Nearest commercial airport Salina (23 miles).
Climate   Average temperatures July 26C ((78F); January 2C (28F).
            Average annual rainfall 34" Often very heavy thunderstorms.
            Occasional droughts, tornadoes and cyclones.
Elevation   1295 feet above sea level.
Local press Salina Journal, 333 S. Fourth St., Salina, KS.67402.
Zip   67463

Information provided by Lavonne Geist, Dickinson County Historical Society and Lynda Lowry, Abilene Area Chamber of Commerce.

MANCHESTER, KANSAS
(Dickinson County)

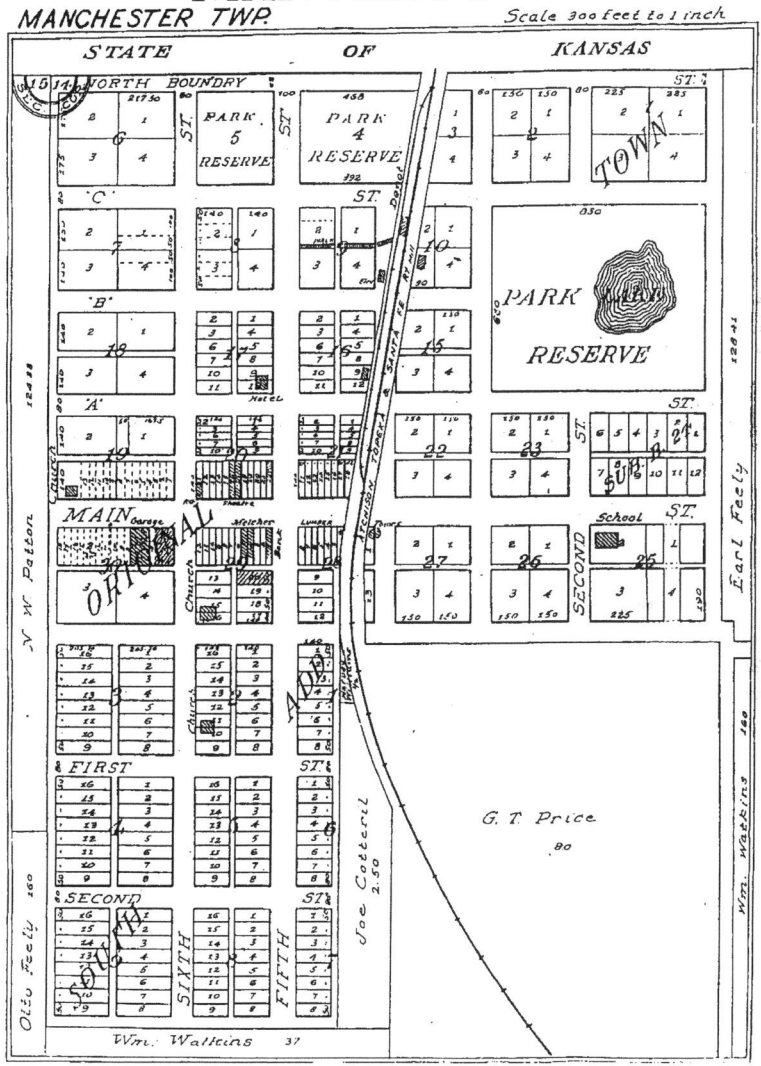

Manchester, Kansas, illustrating the typical
"grid iron" layout of American towns

MANCHESTERKENTUCKY
(Clay County)

Location   Latitude 37.09N. Longitude 83.45W.
County Seat, on Goose Creek, a tributary of the Kentucky River in the foothills of the Appalachian Mountains. 20 miles east of Interstate 75.

Population   1738

The first European settler, James Collins, came to the area in 1798 and he is credited with discovering a salt spring when following a buffalo trail. However, it was apparent by the presence of a large burial ground and other artefacts that the Native Americans had long known of the spring. Most of region at this time was a vast wilderness, exclusively occupied by Native Americans, apart from a few scattered forts which offered little protection to the first European settlers. James White, quartermaster of General Cox's army, saw the potential of the salt spring and purchased all the surrounding land. Soon the salt was being commercially marketed and by 1846 fifteen furnaces produced 200,000 bushels per year. The salt was said to be of exceptionally fine quality which may help account for the longevity of many of the local inhabitants; Solomon Bochart reputedly lived to be 125 years old, John Gilbert to 115, with other centenarians being recorded! The town was known as the "Athens of the West" which reflected the prosperity and culture of the inhabitants at the time.

In May 1807 the Clay County Court authorised the location of a new County Seat on a ten-acre tract of land near the Lower Goose Creek Salt Works. The Court also stipulated that it should be named Greenville after General Green Clay, surveyor of the region, legislator and hero of the War of 1812 against Britain. However, confusion arose with another Greenville in Kentucky and therefore in December 1807 the name was changed to Manchester. The reason for the choice of the name Manchester is unclear but there is some suggestion that it was hoped that the new town would become as prosperous as the English industrial city of that name. However, during the Civil War, in an attempt to deny the Confederacy access to the salt, the wells were destroyed by Union troops and have never been reopened. Because of transport difficulties the growth of the town was slow, reaching only 150 inhabitants by the 1880's and the area remained basically rural.

The Clay County area is also famous, or perhaps more correctly infamous, for the family feuds which continued from generation to generation and resulted in many deaths. The most notorious was that between the Garrard family and the White-Howard clan, although other families were also drawn in. On opposing sides in the Civil War, the family bitterness continued for half a century. In 1898 the Garrards ambushed and killed three of the opposing clan over the alleged theft of timber. The Whites

MANCHESTER, KENTUCKY
(Clay County)

soon retaliated, killing one Garrard and wounding three others. The following year the families indulged in a "Wild West" shoot out in the streets of Manchester but there is no record of the casualties. The feud erupted again in 1901 when the families exchanged shots within the Manchester courthouse and in 1904 another outbreak led to two further fatalities.

The development of the local coal industry led to the arrival of the Louisville and Nashville Railroad in 1914 and by 1966 over a million tons a year were being transported. The coal industry has now declined though some mines still operate. Oil is also produced, albeit in small quantities, approximately 6000 barrels a year. Agriculture remains an important part of the local economy together with hardwood timber. Other local industries include small electrical appliances, metal furniture and upholstered furniture. The building of a new Federal prison in Manchester, completed in 1992, provides work for over 350 full-time employees.

Manchester and Clay County lie almost entirely within the Daniel Boone National Forest and contain some of the most beautiful woodlands and mountain scenery in the state of Kentucky. A mansion in Manchester is said to be the inspiration for the sumptuous mansion Tara in the film "Gone with the Wind" (1930). An elected Mayor and six elected Council Members administer the town.

Transport links

Road	The Daniel Boone Parkway (US 421) gives access to Interstate 75.
Rail	Branch line service for coal industry.
Air	London-Corbin airport 23 miles west of Manchester (6000 ft. runway). Nearest scheduled commercial air service is at Bluegrass Airport (99 miles northwest, near Lexington).
Climate	Summer high July 85.5F. low 62.6F. Average mid 70'sF. Winter- high January 43.8F. low 20.4F. Average mid 30'sF.
Rainfall	Average annual 47.29 inches. Snowfall 12 inches.
Elevation	451 feet above sea level.
Zip code	40962
Local press	The Manchester Enterprise, Ed. Mark Hoskins, 103 3rd St, Manchester, KY. 40962. Tel. (606) 598-6174. Clay County News, Paul Hensley, Pub., Bridge St., Manchester, KY. 40962. Tel. (607) 598-1782.
Reference	"A Brief History of Kentucky and Its Counties", Lloyd G. Lee (Kentucky Imprints, Berea, Kentucky).

MANCHESTER, KENTUCKY
(Clay County)

Reference   "History of Kentucky" Lewis Collins, Kentucky Historical Society, 1966.

"The Kentucky Encyclopedia", Ed. John E. Kleber (University Press of Kentucky).

"Kentucky Place Names", Robert M. Rennick (University Press of Kentucky).

Also in Kentucky - Manchester Islands (Lewis County) and Manchester Branch, a stream in Fayette County.

Information provided by Nancy Lee Smith, Director, Clay County Public Library.

MANCHESTER, LOUISIANA
(Calcasieu County)

Location   Latitude 30.11N. Longitude 93.05W.

Three miles due east of Lake Charles on Highway 397.

Population   "Populated place" US Census 1990 - no figures given.

Located in the south-western corner of Louisiana close to Lake Charles, Manchester (also known as Gene) appears to be too small to appear on any but the most detailed of maps. The region is sub-tropical, being only 34 miles from the Gulf of Mexico. The area is noted for its many flowers. It is said that the pirate Jean Lafitte hid some of his plundered treasure in the Lake Charles area.

Transport links

Road   On Highway 397 just south of US Interstate 10.

Air   Lake Charles Airport 3 miles.

Water   Port of Lake Charles (deep water harbour).

Climate   Generally humid, sub-tropical with maritime character.

Mild temperatures with few extremes.

Annual rainfall 53.03 inches. Average temperatures January (normal) 60.8F. July (normal) 91.0F.

Elevation   20 feet above sea level (average).

Zip(s)   70601-70669

Local Press   American Press, P.O.Box 2893, Lake Charles, LA.70602.

Information via Internet.

MANCHESTER, MAINE
(Kennebec County)
"The Queue City of Maine"

Location   Latitude 44.19N. Longitude 69.51W.
           A small town in the Kennebec Valley area of S.E.Maine, at the
           intersection of US Route 202 and State Highway 17. State
           Capital Augusta (4 miles).
Population   2465

Europeans first settled the area around the 1770's when it was known as Hallowell Cross Roads on the "Coos" trail (named after the Cohoses Indians). Farmers travelled this trail with their produce from northern New Hampshire and northwest Maine to the market town of Hallowell on the Kennebec River. A reminder of these pioneering days is a marker stone found in Manchester inscribed *"5 M To K RIVER"*.

The present town of Manchester was incorporated in 1850 under the name of Kennebec and three selectmen and a town treasurer were elected to run the town. In the following April ten cents an hour was voted for men to work on the roads in winter and twelve cents for men and oxen in summer. By 1852 the town had a school and the following year a Town Hall.

In 1854 a Town Meeting instructed the selectmen to petition the State Legislature to change the name of the town to Manchester. The reason for this change of name is unknown but it was not uncommon for small towns to undergo several name changes during the course of their development. In 1855 $85 was voted to buy a town hearse! In the 1860 election the townsfolk voted solidly for U.S. President Abraham Lincoln who received 135 of the 155 votes cast.

At the outbreak of the Civil War in 1861 a Town Meeting voted to give $1.50c. a week to any family whose man was in military service. This was followed in 1862 by the vote of a $75 bounty to each citizen who enlisted, later raised to $125, a considerable sum of money in those days. Not surprisingly by 1865, the last year of the war, the town had to borrow money at 8% interest to defray the cost of recruiting soldiers.

The town has developed little over the years and continues to provide limited services for the surrounding, mainly agricultural, area. The principle local crop is apples. There is no industrialisation, new development being mainly housing for the elderly. The main town events are an annual Master Festival held in July and antique shows which are held at intervals throughout the year. The Township of Manchester, which includes the town of Manchester, is one of the former civil administrative areas of Kennebec County.

Manchester came to international attention in December 1982 when ten years old Samantha Smith, a local schoolgirl, wrote to the Russian Prime

MANCHESTER, MAINE
(Kennebec County)

Minister, Yuri Andropov. In her letter she confided her fears for the future in the light of the tense relations between the USA and Russia. The Russian Premier responded by inviting Samantha and her family to visit Russia to meet Russian children and learn more about the country. Tragically Samantha was killed in a plane crash in 1985 but her statue in Atlanta, the State capital, commemorates her peace initiative.

Transport links

Road	5 miles east of US Interstate Highway 95.
Rail	Augusta (4 miles).
Air	Augusta State Airport (5 miles) - North West Airlink.
Climate	Long, cold winters, average 20F; short, cool summers average 75F. Rainfall moderate, 40 inches.
Elevation	47 feet above sea level.
Local press	Kennebec Journal, 274 Western Avenue, Augusta, Maine 04330. Tel. (207) 623 3811.
Zip	04351
Reference	"Manchester 1775-1975" Manchester Bicentennial Committee. "Dictionary of Maine Place Names", Phillip R. Rutherford.

Also in Maine - Manchester Point (Hancock County) on the Atlantic coast near Ellsworth.

Information provided by Melora Macbeth, Charles M. Bailey Public Library, Winthrop, Maine and Susan Smith, Kennebec Valley Chamber of Commerce Information Services.

The Samantha Smith Memorial, Manchester, Maine
(Picture courtesy of Kennebec Valley Chamber of Commerce)

MANCHESTER, MARYLAND
(Carroll County)

Location   Latitude 39.39 N. Longitude 76.53 W.
On Highway 30 near the State boundary with Pennsylvania.
Baltimore 28 miles, Washington, DC, 50 miles.
Population   3329

The town of Manchester stands at the intersection of original Native American trails connecting the Potomac and Susquehanna rivers and between Baltimore and Hanover. Native Americans of the Susquehannock tribe, *"the most noble and heroic Indians that dwell in the confines of America"* (Alsop), continued to use the trails until the mid 18th century. The first recorded land grant in the Manchester area came in 1737 when 150 acres was granted to an Englishman, Samuel Stevens. This grant was known as "Steven's Hope", which became "McGill's Choice" on its sale to Andrew McGill in 1744. Other land grants in the area were given individual names; "Ely's Rock", "Abraham's Garden", "Adam's Choice" and so on.

The site of Manchester was first settled in 1758 when a twenty-five acre tract was granted to "German Churche", the actual church being built in 1760. This was unusual in the fact that the church, which served the surrounding farms, was built before the land was settled. A log schoolhouse was erected next to the church in 1762 in which reading and writing were taught in English and German *"but the German language shall have precedence because our congregation is a German congregation and the schoolhouse is its property."* No beating about the bush in those days!

Manchester, Maryland Town Crest
(Courtesy of Manchester, Maryland Historical Center)

MANCHESTER, MARYLAND
(Carroll County)

On the 5th March 1765 a tract of 67 acres of land adjoining "German Churche" was surveyed and patented to Captain Richard Richards in a grant known as "New Market". Richards laid out a new town on his grant, naming it after his hometown of Manchester, England. Richards laid out 122 lots each approximately 80 feet by 130 feet of irregular shape, due to the fact that the German Church lands occupied a v-shaped portion of the site of the new town. These original lots were leased not sold and some are still subject to ground rent today. The site was well chosen and the town quickly became settled. Sons-in-law of Richard Richards founded the nearby towns of Hampstead and Westminster.

By the middle of the 18th century German settlers began to arrive in large numbers, so much so that the primary language of the town became German. Their love of noodles gave the town the nickname "Noodle Doosey" and later "Gingercake Town" for a similar reason. Indeed, a community just west of the town was known as Germantown before being absorbed into Manchester in 1834 when the town was incorporated.

The act of incorporation stipulated the limits of the town as extending *"one quarter mile each way of the tavern owned by David Everhart."* A new school, required to serve the needs of the growing population, was opened in 1831. This school became the "Manchester Academy" in 1835, the curriculum being *"orthography* (correct spelling), *algebra, mensuration, surveying, Euclid's elements of geometry, grammar, geography, history, natural philosophy, chemistry, Latin, Greek, moral science, rhetoric, moral philosophy and metaphysics."* Modern education appears very limited in comparison! The school was fee paying ($2 a quarter) but these were waived for the children of the poor or could be paid in kind, by washing, sewing or supplying firewood, etc.

The building of the turnpike road in 1807 opened up trade between Baltimore and Pittsburgh and led to the growth of the town. Huge Conestoga wagons, "schooners of the desert", familiar today to devotees of cowboy films, drawn by six or eight horses, passed continually through the town along the turnpike and taverns and stores opened to meet the needs of the drivers. Soon the stagecoach was making regular runs with stops at Manchester, ending in 1879 when the railroad arrived at nearby Greenmount. The citizens of Manchester had hoped and planned for the coming of the railroad only for the town to be by-passed by the railroad company. It was widely held that graft had steered the railroad away from Manchester but, whatever the reason, the railroad did not come and its citizens had to take the stage to Greenmount to catch a train to Baltimore. This failure to attract the railroad had a major adverse effect on the future development of Manchester.

MANCHESTER, MARYLAND
(Carroll County)

Industry first came to Manchester in the mid 19th century in the form of the Manchester Foundry and Machine Works. It manufactured a variety of iron castings. The machinery was at first driven by a team of six horses harnessed to six arms radiating from a central capstan where the "driver" sat. The horses were later replaced by two steam engines that between them generated 15 horsepower.

As tobacco was a major crop in the Manchester area the making of cigars (or segars as they were known) also became an important industry, at one time employing upwards of two hundred workers. Two popular brands were "Happy Thoughts" and "Old Smoker's Delight". This industry died out in the 1930's when machinery replaced the traditional hand rolling method of making cigars. Other industries included coach building, the small scale mining of gold (yes, in 19th century Manchester the streets were "paved with gold"!), brick making and stone quarrying. Because of its favourable elevated position the town began to attract summer visitors in the late 19th century which led to opening of hotels and boarding houses.

Today Manchester still serves the needs of the local community and summer visitors. The pleasant location and ambience of the town has attracted many new residents who commute to work in nearby Hampstead, Hanover, Westminster and Baltimore.

Transport links
Road   On Highway 30, east of US Interstate 83 (13 miles).
Air   Baltimore-Washington International 30 miles.
Climate   No specific figures available. Hot summers, cool winters. Ample rainfall.
Elevation   n/a
Local press Carroll County Times, 201 Railway Avenue, Westminster, MD. 21158-0346.
Zip(s)   21088, 21002.
Also in Maryland - Manchester Estates (Prince George's County) near Camp Springs, south east of Washington DC. Manchester Park (Cecil County) adjacent to Cherry Hill, north of Elkton, in the north east corner of the State, near the border with Eastern Pennsylvania and Delaware. The US Census Bureau indicates both as "populated places" but no figures are given, nor do they appear on maps.
Information provided by Carolyn A. Garber, Carroll County Chamber of Commerce; Julia Berwager, Manchester Md. Historical Center and Manchester Post Office.

A WORLD OF MANCHESTERS

MANCHESTER, MARYLAND
(Carroll County)

A charmingly named park in Manchester, Maryland
(Courtesy of Manchester, Maryland Historical Center)

MANCHESTER-BY-THE SEA, MASSACHUSETTS
(Essex County)

Location   Latitude 42.34N. Longitude 70.47 W.
Northeastern Massachusetts on Cape Ann. Salem 6 miles, Boston 25 miles.
Population   5228

It was their Puritan faith that brought English settlers to Massachusetts, the Pilgrim Fathers in the "Mayflower" establishing their first settlement at Plymouth in 1620. Other pilgrims soon followed and in 1629 the good ship "Talbot", carrying a hundred or more colonists, put into what was to become Manchester harbour on the coast of Cape Ann. The Reverend Francis Higginson wrote in his journal *"a fine sweet harbour where twenty ships may lie and easily ride there"*. Between 1630 and 1643 twenty thousand men, women and children crossed to New England in 200 ships. A number of settlements were established, one of which initially known as Jeffreys Creek, was renamed Manchester in 1645, either after the town in England or possibly in honour of the Duke of Manchester.

Life in the new settlements was dangerous and hard with wolves and rattlesnakes in the woods, attacks by Native Americans and long cold

58

MANCHESTER-BY-THE SEA, MASSACHUSETTS
(Essex County)

winters. The wars in Europe had spilled over into the new colonies and both the French and British recruited Native American allies. The settlements in Massachusetts suffered particularly heavily with sixteen towns being destroyed or abandoned. However, in spite of the hardships and danger, by 1691 Manchester's population had grown to 350 residents. A larger Meeting House was constructed and, at the turn of the century, the village boasted a schoolhouse, tide mill, sawmill and a blacksmith's shop. In 1717 the winter was so bad that Judge Samuel Sewall recorded *"At six o'clock my ink freezes so that I can hardly write by a good fire in my (wife's) chamber"*.

The wars between Britain and France continued intermittently throughout the 18th century and in 1745 men from Manchester took part in the successful attack on the French fort at Louisburg, Nova Scotia, giving England control of the entire coastline. British rule in North America was finally consolidated with the capture of Quebec in 1759.

The outbreak of the Revolutionary War brought mixed loyalties to the inhabitants of Manchester, the town being but thirty miles from Boston, the scene of the famous "Tea Party". Some citizens, loyal to the Crown, fled to New Brunswick or Nova Scotia; others stayed and painted their chimney pots white to demonstrate their loyalty. However, a Town Meeting in 1775 voted in favour of the rebellion and the town provided men, money and supplies for Washington's fledgling army and ships and men for the growing fleet of privateers that harried the British supply lines. But the war was not without cost to the town of Manchester. In one incident eighteen men, including Dr. Joseph Whipple, the town's surgeon, lost their lives when the privateer Gloucester went down. There were many acts of heroism by Manchester men both on sea and on land before the war came to an end and eighty men from the town lost their lives in the conflict.

Recovery from the war took time but by the end of the century Manchester was one of the foremost fishing ports on the Atlantic coast. The men had to take up arms again in 1812 when the United States declared war against Britain in response to British attacks on American ships during the war against Napoleon. Manchester suffered from the British blockade during the war but peace in 1815 brought a restoration of the town's fortunes. By 1845 the town had grown to 1600 and a new industry, furniture making, began to rival fishing as the main source of employment. The railway came in 1847 with two passenger and one freight train each day to Boston. Many of the Irish labourers, who worked on the railway construction, later settled in the town. The outbreak of the Civil War in 1861 saw 159 Manchester men serve the Union cause, sixteen of whom were to lose their lives.

It was during the mid nineteenth century, after the coming of the

MANCHESTER-BY-THE SEA, MASSACHUSETTS
(Essex County)

railroad, that Manchester developed as a summer resort. A number of notable Americans began to build summerhouses in and around the town and Junius Brutus Booth, older brother of Lincoln's assassin John Wilkes Booth, built a "Grand Hotel" in the town. This hotel, the Masconomo House, could seat three hundred people in its dining room. By the end of the century, the town had a golf club and a yacht club.

In 1904 the town counted eleven ambassadors and their entourages among its summer residents and the rich and famous from all nations were regular visitors. A building boom gave employment and brought prosperity to the town as a whole. It led, however, to the creation of two quite different Manchesters, a summer town filled with rich temporary residents living in fine houses and a winter town whose inhabitants struggled to make ends meet.

Although the depression of the 1930's hit Manchester hard, employment was still to be found maintaining the summerhouses, working on the roads and various community projects. The depression gave way to the trials and tribulations of the Second World War in which fifteen Manchester residents gave their lives in the service of their country.

After the war the character of the town was to change for good, new housing estates being built for young families. The summer/winter divide became less pronounced, with commuting to work in nearby Salem or Boston becoming the norm.

The town's population is predicted to remain at around the five and a half thousand level. The town's name was changed to Manchester-by-the-Sea in 1990 as a result of a keenly contested vote at a Town Meeting, though James T. Fields had first suggested the new name as far back as the turn of the century.

The 350th Anniversary Crest Manchester-by-the-Sea
(Courtesy of Town Board)

MANCHESTER-BY-THE SEA, MASSACHUSETTS
(Essex County)

Transport links
Road   On Highway 127 adjacent to State Highway 128.
Rail   Boston & Maine line through Manchester.
Air   Boston International Airport 22 miles.
Climate   Long, cold winters, warm summers. Median temperatures
            25.8F (Jan.), 71.6F (July). Annual rainfall 43.6 inches.
Elevation   30 feet above sea level.
Local press The Manchester Cricket (weekly).
Zip   01944
Reference   "A Brief History of Manchester" Gordon Abbott, Jr. 1995.
            Quoted by Abbott –"History of the Town of Manchester"
            1645-1895, Reverend Darius F. Lamson.
            "Manchester-by-the Sea" Frank L. Floyd, 1945.
            "A History of Twentieth Century Manchester" Benjamin B.
            Merrill, 1990.
            "Boston's North Shore 1823-1890" and "Boston's Gold Coast,
            The North Shore 1890-1929" both published by Little, Brown
            & Co.
            "Builders of the Bay Colony" Samuel Eliot Morison, 1930.
Also in Massachusetts - Manchester Channel, Manchester Bay, Manchester
Harbor, (all Essex County); Manchester Pond (3), reservoirs; Manchester
Dam and Manchester Pond East Dyke (all Bristol County).
Information provided by Betsy Sinnicks, Town Hall, Manchester-by-the-Sea.

MANCHESTER, MICHIGAN
(Washtenaw County)

Location   Latitude 42.09N. Longitude 84.02W.
            Along the River Raisin in south-east Michigan, midway
            between Ann Arbor (15 miles) and Jackson (20 miles).
Population Manchester Village 2160; Manchester Township 4102
        This part of western Washtenaw County was first settled in the 1830's
and chartered as a village in 1867, celebrating its 125th anniversary in 1992.
It is a beautiful area of gentle hills and rich farmland. The village of
Manchester is at the centre of four townships - Manchester, Sharon, Freedom
and Bridgewater. Thus, though the population of Manchester itself is less
than 2000, it forms part of a much larger population in the immediate
surrounding area. The population of the village has remained reasonably
constant over the past twenty-five years. The village library, established
1838, was the first township library in the State of Michigan.

MANCHESTER, MICHIGAN
(Washtenaw County)

The highlight of the town year is the annual Manchester Chicken Broil held on the third Thursday of July. On this day the village population swells to eight times its normal size and 14,000 people enjoy tender chicken halves broiled and butter basted over charcoal. Four specially constructed charcoal fire pits, each 100 feet long, are constructed in which to cook the chickens. The men of the village supervise the broiling and their children act as "butter boys", learning from their fathers ready for the day when they will be called upon to maintain the tradition of the annual Chicken Broil.

The village offers ample recreational facilities including four public parks, golf and swimming in addition to fishing and boating on the River Raisin. Many of the town's nineteenth century buildings remain, including those built in the European style and well preserved examples of the more traditional "country" construction.

Transport links

Road	On Highway 52, 8 miles north of US Federal Highway 12.
Air	Rossettie airport. Nearest commercial airports - Jackson 20 miles and Ann Arbor 15 miles.
Climate	Average temperatures Summer 80F. Winter 32F. Annual rainfall 30.04 inches.
Elevation	918 feet above sea level.
Local press	Manchester Chronicle, Ed. Kathy Kueffner, 201 East Main Street, PO Box 697, Manchester, MI 48158.
	Manchester Enterprise, Ed. Emory Garlick, 109 East Main Street, PO Box 706 Manchester, MI 48158.
	Ann Arbor News, Ed. Rick Fitzgerald, PO Box 1147, Ann Arbor, MI 48106-1147.
Zip Code	48158

Also in Michigan - Manchester School (Kent County).

Information provided by Dianne Schwab, Director, Community Resource Centre, 122 W. Main St., PO Box 433, Manchester, Mi. 48158-0433.

MANCHESTER, MINNESOTA
(Freeborn County)

Location   Latitude 43.32N. Longitude 93.27W.
In south east Minnesota near Iowa border, 6 miles north east of Albert Lea, 26 miles west of Austin.

Population   81 (Manchester Village) 469 (Manchester Township)

Too small to be shown on most maps, Manchester is the name of both a village and a township in Freeborn County, the township being a widely scattered collection of homesteads and the village an "urban" area.

The first recorded European settler was S.S.Skiff, a New Yorker who came to the area on the 6th June 1856, followed a week later by a group of Norwegian settlers who travelled via Iowa. Skiff only remained for two years before departing in 1858 for Wisconsin, which he apparently didn't find to his liking for he returned in 1860.

The first house was erected by Gune Thykeson in June 1856, a log cabin 12x14 feet with a log and sod roof. Evidence that the majority of early settlers were predominantly Norwegian in origin can clearly be seen on the tombstones in the Norwegian Lutheran Cemetery in the town. Indeed, the first name of the town was Olborg after the Norwegian hometown post office of Ole Petersen, one of the early settlers.

The town subsequently went through several changes of name from "Buckeye" (reputedly the nickname of two settlers from Ohio), to "Liberty" in 1858 (rejected by the State Auditor as there were already two other Liberty's in the State) and finally to Manchester in 1859. It is believed that Mathias Anderson, who came from the town of Manchester in Boone County, Illinois, proposed the same name for the new township.

The first town meeting took place in 1858 at which the town officers and officials were elected. This was followed in 1861 with the building of a log schoolhouse large enough for the roll of thirty scholars taught by Emma Walker. The Manchester Post Office was established in the village store in 1878, the first quarter's post office business amounting to $6, rising later to $8.89c. Manchester Village was platted in 1882 by Ole Peterson in section 15 of the township and by 1884 the population had risen to 784. At the turn of the century the township boasted a town hall, a bank, a railroad station (the Minneapolis & St. Louis Railroad) and an hotel.

The town was incorporated in 1947 and mains water came in the same year. A tornado struck in 1952 causing considerable damage, as did a further storm in 1967. The population has remained small in number and today Manchester continues much as it has over the years, a small town serving the needs of the local farming community.

MANCHESTER, MINNESOTA
(Freeborn County)

Transport links
Road   3 miles north of Interstate 90.
Air   Interstate Austin 26 miles; International Minneapolis St.Paul 75 miles.
Climate   Long, cold winters; short summers; moderate rainfall.
Elevation   1283 feet above sea level.
Local press   The Albert Lea Tribune, 808 W. Front St., Albert Lea, MN.56007.
Zip   56064
Reference   "History of Freeborn County", Minnesota Historical Society, 1882.
              "Freeborn County Heritage", Freeborn County, Minnesota Historical & Genealogical Societies, 1988.
Also in Minnesota - Manchester Square, a park on shore of Lake Superior, (St. Louis County).
Information provided by Linda Evenson, Freeborn County Historical Association.

MANCHESTER LANDING, MISSISSIPPI
(Humphreys County)

Location   Latitude 33.07N. Longitude 090.22W.
      An historic river landing on the Yazoo River, probably so named because of its proximity to the town of Manchester (now Yazoo City). The US Census Bureau gives no population figure for the locality.
Elevation   95 feet above sea level.
Information via Internet

NOTICE.
The Steamer **ONTARIO**, R. WILSON, Master, will leave this City for *Hannan's Bluffs* on the 16th of February, so as to accommodate passengers who may wish to attend the sale of lots at Manchester, on the Yazoo river, which will take place on the 22d of February—and will wait until the sale is over.
January 22, 1830.   87-

A steamer trip to the auction of housing plots in Manchester, Mississippi.
112 lots were sold at prices ranging from $75 to $355

MANCHESTER LANDING, MISSISSIPPI
(Humphreys County)

MANCHESTER HOTEL.

Manchester,  Missisippi.

THE subscribers beg leave to inform the public generally, that they have opened a House of Entertainment for the reception of Customers, both single Gentlemen and Families, in the town of Manchester.

Their Stables will be amply supplied with provender for horses, and attended by a faithful ostler. They deem themselves prepared in every respect, to give general satisfaction.

J. T. DORSEY,
WM. PHILLIPS, Jr.

Manchester, May 1st, 1832.   35-4t

Vicksburg Advocate, **May 10, 1832**

A comfortable hotel with entertainment laid on. What more could one want? This Manchester changed its name to Yazoo City in 1839

MANCHESTER, MISSOURI
(St. Louis County)

Location   Latitude 38.35N. Longitude 90.30.
Manchester, Missouri is on the outskirts of the city of St. Louis. It lies on the intersection of Highways 100 and 141.

Population   6447 (1994)

In 1673 Father Jacques Marquette, a Jesuit priest accompanied by Louis Joliet, a native Canadian, explored the vast area below the confluence of the Missouri and Mississippi rivers. They discovered a group of Osage Indians living near a spring. The journal of the explorers described the spring as a place where rival tribes fought for possession of the clear flowing water. This spring was later named "Manchester Spring" presumably for its proximity to the new township of Manchester. The spring still flows and is one of three natural sulphur springs in the area estimated by archaeologists to be 8000 years old. Being on one of the western trails the spring created a

MANCHESTER, MISSOURI
(St. Louis County)

natural stopping place for travellers on their way to Jefferson City to refresh themselves and their animals

Around 1800 Bryson O'Hara built a workshop nearby. He supplied ox yokes, oxbows and axe handles made from local timber. In 1812 settlers began moving into what was known as Bon Homme Township (trans. "Good Man") near the spring and by 1820 the settlement had a blacksmith, store, tannery and tavern. There is evidence of a settlement known as Manchester (from a survey dated 1804), and earlier records of the area indicate *"Louis Solomon Migeron made his appearance in St. Louis County in 1786, and ran a gunsmith shop in Manchester making flintlock rifles by hand."* The small community began to be known as Hoardstown after James Hoard, a large landowner. On his death in 1825 the town was renamed Manchester.

There must have been something of a "frontier town" atmosphere in the early days of the settlement because, in 1834, Elijah P. Lovejoy, the well-known St. Louis abolitionist minister, wrote to his supervisor that Manchester *"its wickedness has acquired the name of Sodom"*. However, by 1837 Manchester had added a Methodist church to its twelve log houses, several business buildings and a school. Throughout the 19th century most settlers made their living as farmers, selling their crops in St. Louis.

Although missing out to nearby Valley Park on a railroad connection, Manchester continued to expand with new industries such as a brewery, gristmill, cigar maker, soda water factory and construction company.

During the Civil War the Union Army had a camp at Manchester Spring. By 1894 there were two public halls, one of which, the Lyceum, was in turn used as a tin shop, theatre, grocery & dry goods store, ice cream and soda parlour, movie theatre and post office. The municipal authorities finally purchased the building in 1979. It was moved back 40 feet from its original site for road widening, restored and now has a new lease of life as the City Hall. The Lyceum City Hall appears in the city logo (see page 67) with the motto "A Proud Past, A Bright Future".

After the Second World War Manchester attracted extensive residential development and was incorporated as a village in 1951. The need to provide water and sewage to the new developments caused financial problems, as villages were limited in the amount of money they could borrow from the state or federal government. Therefore, on 17th August 1959, Manchester elected to become a fourth-class city, which gave greater bonding and borrowing facilities.

The modern city of Manchester has a population of 6,447 within an area of just over two square miles. It is governed by a Mayor and Board of Alderman assisted by a full-time professional administrator. The city has

MANCHESTER, MISSOURI
(St. Louis County)

an attractive downtown Historic District where a number of historically or architecturally significant buildings, dating from 1840 to 1912, have been preserved. There are also many commercial, office and retail businesses and comprehensive recreational facilities. The old Indian trail to the Mississippi River, which later formed a major part of the wagon trail heading west, is now the five lane Highway 100 known as Manchester Road. A highlight of the year is the annual "Manchester Homecoming" and the Mardi Gras parade and fair held every September.

"A PROUD PAST   A BRIGHT FUTURE"

The Town Crest features the elegant Lyceum

The real Lyceum, former theatre
and now the City Hall.
(Pictures courtesy of the City of Manchester)

MANCHESTER, MISSOURI
(St. Louis County)

Transport links
Road   On the intersection of Highways 100 and 141.
Rail   Nearest rail link St.Louis, 20 miles.
Air   Lambert-St. Louis International Airport (15miles).
Climate   Average Temperatures Summer 80-85F, Winter 30-40F.
Elevation   755 feet above sea level.
Local press St. Louis Post Dispatch, 900 North Tucker Blvd.,
            St. Louis, MO. 63101. Tel. 314-340-8888.
            Suburban Journals, 1714 Deer Tracks, St. Louis, Mo. 63101.
            Tel. 314-821-1110.
Zip   63011
Reference   "Where We Live" Missouri Historical Society, 1994.
Also in Missouri – Manchester, a locality in Kansas City (Jackson County)
and the historic Manchester Lead Diggings (St. Francois County).
Information provided by Michael B. Leavitt and Barbara J. Burns, City
Administrators, City of Manchester, 14318 Manchester Road, Manchester,
Missouri 63011.

A roadside welcome to Manchester, Missouri
(Picture courtesy of the City of Manchester)

MANCHESTER, MONTANA
(Cascade County)

Location   Latitude 47.32N. Longitude 111.27W.
Railroad station and site of an historic school and post office.
On US Interstate Highway 15, northwest outskirts of Great Falls.
Population Populated place – The US Census Bureau gives no figure.

The history of Montana reflects that of the other western American states in that European settlement came mainly in the latter part of the nineteenth century with the discovery of gold and the development of the railroads. Prior to this the main white presence in the region was limited to fur trappers, particularly beaver trappers; Manuel Lisa establishing the first fur trading post in 1807. By the 1840's, the fur trade had declined and cattle became important.

The discovery of gold in the 1850's inevitably led to conflict over land with the Native Americans culminating, in 1876, in the Battle of the Little Big Horn, "Custer's Last Stand". The Sioux, under Chiefs Sitting Bull and Crazy Horse, annihilated Custer's force of US cavalry. Concurrent with the Native American conflict was the conflict over grazing rights between the cattle barons and newly arrived sheep farmers. The unsettled times were reflected in the great lawlessness of the period; one group of outlaws, the Plummer gang, reputedly being responsible for more than one hundred deaths before most were rounded up and hanged.

Situated on the flat and gently rolling Great Plains of Montana the origins of the small settlement of Manchester have long been forgotten or lost, (if they were ever considered important enough to be recorded). It would appear to be one of the many small settlements that grew around a railroad stop serving the surrounding community, with a post office, school and general store. Today it is simply listed as a "populated place" by US Census Bureau with no figure given indicating that the number of inhabitants is probably below one hundred.

Transport links
Road   US Interstate Highway 15.
Air   Great Falls International Airport.
Climate   Average temperatures July high 86F. January high 31F.
Great climatic extremes. Lowest recorded temperature -57C (-70F), highest 47C (+117F). Annual average rainfall 14 inches; snowfall 56 inches.
Elevation 3353 feet above sea level.
Local press Cascade Courier, 100 First St. N., Cascade, MT. 59421.
Zip Codes n/a
Information via Internet

MANCHESTER PRECINCT, NEBRASKA
(Boone County)

Location   Latitude 41.69N. Longitude 98.00W.
            Near Albion on Highway 14.
Population 2275 (North Manchester Precinct); 355 (Southeast Manchester
            Precinct); 294 (Southwest Manchester Precinct)
        Situated near Beaver Creek on the outskirts of Albion, Manchester
Precinct appears to be a general locality rather than a specific town or
village. The first European settlers arrived in the area in 1871 and legend has
it that the name Albion came about through a game of euchre, a card game
popular in America in the late 1800's. The winner named the new settlement
Albion but granted the loser the honour of naming the precinct (district). The
sensible chap chose the name Manchester. It does not appear on maps and all
research and enquiries have failed to provide any further information. Apart
from an entry in the 1990 US Census it seems for all intents and purposes not
to exist!
Transport links
Road   On Highway 14.
Air   Airports at Norfolk (45 miles) and Grand Island (70 miles).
Climate   Dry continental, cold winters hot summers. Severe storms
            common, occasional drought years. Average temperatures –
            July 78F (26C), January 20F (-7C). Annual average rainfall
            30"; Snowfall 32".
Elevation   n/a
Local Press Norfolk Daily News, 525 Norfolk Av., Norfolk, NE 68702.
Zip   68620
Information via Internet

MANCHESTER, NEW HAMPSHIRE
(Hillsborough County)

Location   Latitude 42.59N. Longitude 71.27W.
            South-central New Hampshire. The State's largest city and the
            centre of a metropolitan area comprising of the City of
            Manchester and the towns of Allenstown, Auburn, Bedford,
            Candia, Goffstown, Hookset, Londonderry and Weare. The
            Merrimack River bisects the city.
Population 107,006 (City of Manchester 2000); 173,907 (Manchester
            Metropolitan Area 1994) Over half a million people live within
            a twenty-mile radius of Manchester.
        The site of Manchester was originally Namoskeag, Native American
for *"place of much fish"*. Archaeologists have traced human settlements in

70

MANCHESTER, NEW HAMPSHIRE
(Hillsborough County)

the Merrimack River valley area going back over ten thousand years but by 1725 most of the Native Americans had moved northwards to escape the conflict and disease brought by European settlers. In 1722-3, Scots and Irish immigrants began to settle in the area bringing with them their skills in wool spinning and weaving. First known as Old Harry's Town, after one of the original settlers, it became Tyngstown after 1735 when the Massachusetts Bay Colony granted it to Capt. William Tyng's men. In 1771 it was incorporated as the town of Derryfield.

Having seen the usefulness of the barge canals in Manchester, England, Samuel Blodget sought to emulate them by constructing a canal and lock system around the Amoskeag Falls in the Merrimack River. Construction, begun in 1794, took thirteen years, being completed in 1807. Blodget's canal, together with the Middlesex canal in Massachusetts, opened water navigation to Boston and Concord. In 1810, three years after Blodget's death, Derryfield voted to change its name to honour his prediction that *"a city like unto Manchester, England"* would rise because of the waterpower of the Amoskeag Falls.

In 1828 a group of Boston investors known as The Boston Associates purchased the rights to the waterpower at the falls and planned a complex of mills. This became the Amoskeag Manufacturing Company which, at its peak, employed 17,000 workers in a mill yard of over 30 major mills with eight million feet of floor space - the largest textile company in the world. By 1906 the mills were producing four million yards of cloth per week. Until the 1930's the town's economy depended almost exclusively on the Amoskeag Manufacturing Company's cotton milling operations and Manchester was a company town in every sense of the word. However, the worldwide depression of the 1930's, and increasing competition from southern mills and labour problems, forced the company to close in 1936. A Citizens' Committee purchased the mill complex and set about attracting new industries to the town including shoes and leather goods, rubber, automobile accessories, electrical instruments and paper manufacture.

Today Manchester has a diverse economy of manufacturing, service and retail companies and is the financial and commercial centre for northern New England. Places of interest include the Currier Gallery of Art (permanent collection of American fine and decorative art), the Manchester Institute of Arts and Sciences (exhibitions and courses), the Centre Franco-Americaine (the culture, heritage and history of the French in North America) and the Palace Theatre (drama, dance and orchestral concerts). The city also has two fine orchestras, the New Hampshire Philharmonic and the New Hampshire Symphony. Recreational activities include water sports,

MANCHESTER, NEW HAMPSHIRE
(Hillsborough County)

golf, tennis, hunting, ice-skating and skiing.

Transport links

Road	Interstate 293 (the Frederick E. Everett Turnpike) and Inter - state 93 encircle Manchester. 17 miles from State Capital Concord, 58 miles from Boston.
Rail	Boston and Maine Railroad.
Air	Manchester Airport - regional services to major hubs through - out the US. A new terminal opened in 1994.
Water	Portsmouth (46 miles). Container port, year round deep-water harbour.
Climate	Average temperatures Summer 70F(July); Winter 47F. Annual rainfall average 40.56 ins. Annual snowfall average 60.6 inches.
Elevation	110/510 feet above sea level.
Local press	Union Leader (Daily), New Hampshire Sunday News, Boston Globe/NH Weekly (Sunday). Manchester Magazine (monthly), BNH Magazine (monthly)
Zip(s)	03100-4; 03107-8.
Reference	"Fingertip Facts", Manchester Economic Development Office, 1985.

Also in New Hampshire - Manchester Speedway (Rockingham County).

Information provided by Greater Manchester Chamber of Commerce.

Red Man's Pow Wow - Manchester, New Hampshire April 1916
(the event was held for three days)
(Picture courtesy of Greater Manchester Chamber of Commerce)

MANCHESTER, NEW HAMPSHIRE
(Hillsborough County)

Victory Park in downtown Manchester, New Hampshire
(Picture courtesy of Greater Manchester Chamber of Commerce)

MANCHESTER, NEW JERSEY
(Ocean County)

Location   Latitude 39.96N. Longitude 74.37W.
On Highway 70, near Brown Mills.
Population   Manchester Township 38,928 (2000); Lakehurst Borough
(formally Manchester Village) 3078 (1990)

The original Native American inhabitants of this part of North America were obviously people with a very literal turn of mind for they called themselves Lenni-Lanape, meaning "original people" - a much more descriptive term than the rather prosaic Delaware Indians as they came to be known by the white settlers. The first European contact came in 1524 when the Florentine Giovanni da Verrazzona explored the area for the French King Francis I. As Verrazzona sailed along the coast, he saw *"everywhere very great fires by reason of the multitude of the inhabitants"*. Verrazzona made only brief landings, one probably at the mouth of the Hudson River,

Almost a century later in 1609, and again in 1618, the English explorer Henry Hudson explored the coast and the Hudson River, (named after him), in his unsuccessful search for a northwest passage to the Orient. The Dutch soon followed establishing the first trading post settlements including New Amsterdam, later renamed New York. Hard on their heels came Swedish settlers only to be driven out by the Dutch who, in their turn, lost their settlements to the British in 1664. European settlements began to spread inland over the next two centuries; the settlers keen to take advantage of the abundant natural resources in the region.

In the late 1780's, the settlement that was to become Manchester grew around the site of an iron forge known as the Federal Furnace which

MANCHESTER, NEW JERSEY
(Ocean County)

produced pig iron. The locality had deposits of iron ore, an abundant supply of timber for charcoal, and a plentiful water supply. The extensive area of pine forest also led to construction of many water powered saw mills.

The actual origin of the township and the village of Manchester dates from the purchase in 1841, of land in the area by two English settlers, Timothy Wiggins, a merchant from London, and William Hurry from Manchester, England. Hurry had established himself as a New York banker and made the purchase as a Trustee acting on behalf of Adeline Torrey, wife of William Torrey, at the behest of her father, Samuel Whitmore. It was Adeline's husband William Torrey, who founded and named the village and township Manchester, possibly at William Hurry's instigation, in recognition of Hurry's hometown in England.

The Torrey's, with their five sons, moved in 1841 from New York to Manchester. Perhaps it had something to do with the air in Manchester but Adeline Torrey was to give birth to five more children in their new home, all girls, to complement the five sons she brought with her! Torrey proved to be a resourceful and very successful businessman, earning the sobriquet "King of the Pines" for turning the vast forest of pines into charcoal that was much in demand by eastern manufactories at the time. He also established a sawmill to provide cut timber for the construction of houses in the new village.

Such was the progress of his new enterprise that by 1842, only a year after his arrival in Manchester, he built a rail track for wagons of charcoal to be transported to the Toms River for onward transport to the east. However, his attempt to use a steam locomotive brought over from Manchester, England, ended in failure when a bridge on the track proved unable to sustain the weight of the engine. The bridge was for a long time afterwards known as "Iron Bridge" in relation to the iron monster which toppled over when attempting to cross. As a result of this set back, Torrey had to turn to less powerful but more lightweight mule teams to pull the wagons.

In 1865, Torrey and his son William planned a steam railroad that would link New York City with Norfolk, Virginia. The stage wagons in use at the time took five days to complete the journey from New York to Philadelphia. Their Raritan and Delaware Railroad Company linked Port Monmouth on Raritan Bay with Delaware Bay, passing en route through Manchester and other towns. The line would combine with barging on the Raritan and Delaware Bays. Torrey built a brickyard in Manchester using local clay to provide bricks for railway buildings.

To satisfy the demands of local people for local government, Manchester Township formally came into existence on the 6th April 1865.

MANCHESTER, NEW JERSEY
(Ocean County)

The new Township was an administrative area covering 84 square miles of scattered small settlements, including the village of Manchester. The Township's 1084 inhabitants included many men recently returned from fighting on the Union side in the Civil War. However, the decline in the demand for charcoal towards the end of the nineteenth century and the march of progress in the twentieth, which by-passed Manchester, contributed to the decline of the once thriving village.

The village of Manchester was renamed in 1897 when the US Post Office Department changed its name to Lakehurst, though the name of Manchester survives to this day as an administrative area with its own school system, police force and township officials.

In May 1937, Lakehurst became the centre of world attention when the gigantic German airship, the "Hindenburg", caught fire and exploded approaching the US Naval Air Station, killing 37 of the 97 people on board. This disaster, caught on film and shown world wide, marked the end of hydrogen filled airships as a commercial proposition.

Today the Lakehurst area is popular with retired people who make up many of the small communities. The 1990 population age census for Manchester Township showed a great predominance of over sixties, the median age being 68.2 but there are some new housing developments for younger families. Land use is mainly for residential purposes with very little commercial or industrial activity being carried on within the township.

Transport links
Road   US Federal Highway 70.
Air   Lakehurst airport.
Climate   Humid, continental climate, with warm summers and cold winters. Average rainfall of forty inches.
Elevation   Coastal plain below 100 feet above sea level.
Local press n/a
Zip   08759
Reference   "Ocean County, Four Centuries in the Making" Pauline Miller (Ocean County Cultural & Heritage Commission).
            "Place Names of Ocean County, New Jersey, 1609-1849" Vivian Zinkin.
            "Profile of Manchester Township" Ocean County Planning Dept. Jan. 1998.

Information provided by Louise Jane Brown, Ocean County Library and Pauline S. Miller, Ocean County Cultural & Heritage Commission.

MANCHESTER, NEW MEXICO
(Lincoln County)

Location   Latitude 33.42N. Longitude 105.45W.
             Located high in the Capitan Mountains.
Population   Deserted settlement

So remote is this Manchester that the location co-ordinates given by US Government Agencies are only approximations. Set in a sparsely populated area in the heart of the Capitan mountain range, near White Oaks, Manchester would appear today to be nothing more than the historical name for a locality, although the short-lived "Manchester Historical Post Office" (open from June to October 1881) is still listed. It is likely that the town came and went with the gold boom in this part of New Mexico.

White Oaks, of which Manchester may well have been a near neighbour, has a fascinating history. In the 1880's, according to legend, John Wilson, an escaped prisoner from Texas, whilst on the run discovered gold on Baxter Mountain which led to a gold rush to this part of New Mexico. White Oaks became a boom town, at its peak in the 1890's having over 4000 inhabitants, four newspapers, three churches, two hotels, a bank and various saloons and other businesses. However, speculators had pushed up land prices so much that, in 1896, the planned El Paso and Northeastern railroad by-passed White Oaks and followed a less costly route through nearby Carrizozo. With no railroad, White Oaks declined until by the 1950's it had become a virtual ghost town. However, some buildings have recently been restored and it is said to be an interesting place to visit.

This part of New Mexico, particularly the nearby village of Lincoln, is also known as Billy the Kid country, famous for its connection with the most notorious outlaw of all times in the American West. Billy, real name Henry McCarthy, was a working cowboy in Lincoln County and he almost certainly herded his cattle over the ranges on which the settlement of Manchester was to be established. He became involved in a dispute that broke out between groups of local ranchers, the so-called "Lincoln County War", and was arrested, convicted of murder and sentenced to be hanged. He escaped from custody, killing two deputies in the process, and went on the run with a price on his head. Billy was to enjoy only three short months of freedom before being tracked down and killed by Sheriff Pat Garrett in Fort Sumner. Though folklore credits Billy with as many as twenty killings, he is known to have killed *only* four people in his life.

The Manchester location is a few miles east of Roswell which has achieved worldwide fame as being the site of a claimed alien spacecraft landing in 1947. The US Airforce is said to have recovered the bodies of extra-terrestrial life forms but covered up the incident. It is also alleged by many ufologists that details of the "Roswell Incident" are classified as a

MANCHESTER, NEW MEXICO
(Lincoln County)

State Secret and passed on to each new President of the United States.
Transport links

Road   On Highway 349 off State Highway 54.
Air   Albuquerque International Airport (100 miles).
Climate   January19-45F, July 47-82F. Annual Rainfall 23 inches.
            Annual Snowfall 47 inches.
Elevation   6580 feet above sea level.
Local press Roswell Daily Record, PO Box 1897, Roswell, NM 88201.
            Tel. (505) 622 7710.
            Albuquerque Journal, 7777 Jefferson St. NE, Albuquerque,
            NM 87109 4360.Tel. (505) 823 3800.
Zip Code   n/a
Information via Internet

MANCHESTER, NEW YORK STATE
(Ontario County)
'The center of the megalopolis'

Location   Latitude 42.58N. Longitude 77.13W.
            Finger Lakes resort region, west central New York State. On
            outlet of Lake Canandaigua. Off State Highway 90 (New York
            State Thruway). Rochester 22 miles, Syracuse 55 miles.
Population   Manchester Village 1475; Manchester Township (including
            Manchester Center) 9258

This part of the United States began to be settled by Europeans after the Hartford Treaty of 1786. This Treaty settled the conflicting claims of New York and Massachusetts to the vast area of Iraquois land bounded by the Great Lakes to the north and east and Pennsylvania to the south. The following year, 1787, Oliver Phelps negotiated the Treaty of Buffalo Creek which ended the Iraquois claim to the eastern section and opened up over two million acres for settlement. Phelps and his partner Nathaniel Gorhan surveyed the area, divided it into ranges and townships and opened a land office in Canandaigua which is about ten miles south of present day Manchester. The fertile land, temperate climate and low land prices immediately attracted settlers, mainly from New York and New England.

In 1793 the first claims to be staked in the Manchester area were made by Stephen Jared, Joel Phelps and Joab Gillet. Other pioneers soon followed to settle on the site of what was officially known as Township 12, Range 2. The settlement thrived and by 1800 it had a school and a blacksmith's shop. It distinguished itself in the War of 1812 by sending

MANCHESTER, NEW YORK STATE
(Ontario County)

twenty men to fight the British. "Township 12" formed part of the town of Farmington for local administrative purposes and agitation developed for the creation of a separate town. This proposal was voted down at several town meetings. Therefore, in 1821, a group of local residents secretly contacted the New York State Legislature and arranged for the town to be legally separated from Farmington - without telling the people of Farmington!

The "new" town was officially named Burt in the bill in honour of the legislator who pushed it through the State Legislature. However, the new name proved unpopular so the following year, 1822, the town was renamed Manchester - why this name was chosen is unknown. Manchester became the collective name for a number of villages in the area - Clifton Springs, Shortsville, Manchester, Manchester Center, Port Gibson, Plainsville and Littleville. They all flourished throughout the nineteenth century with an economy based on agriculture with some manufacturing such as grain drills in Shortsville. Manchester was incorporated as a village in 1892.

The real turning point for Manchester, as with many American towns at the time, was the coming of the railroad. In November 1891 the Lehigh Railroad was completed and several passenger trains stopped each day at Manchester. It soon became an important rail marshalling yard which, at its peak after World War 1, employed 1,600 people. However, again typical of many small towns, the decline of the rail system in the twentieth century was reflected by a corresponding decline in the town's economy.

Manchester became what it is today; a small, quiet town, one of the many dotted about the beautiful Finger Lakes region. An unusual feature of the town's main street is a jet fighter on display which has become the town's "mascot". Also on Main St. is a large Victorian house, many similar examples of which can still be seen in Manchester, England.

The town's major claim to fame is its association with the founding of the Mormon Church - the Church of Jesus Christ of Latter-day Saints. The family of Joseph Smith (1805-44), the founder of the Mormons, moved to Palmyra close to Manchester when Joseph was eleven years old. In 1827, according to Smith, God directed him to Cumorah Hill near Manchester. There he dug up the Golden Plates on which was written a history of the Native Americans. This history formed the basis of his "Book of Mormon" published in Palmyra in 1830, the same year that Smith founded his new church in Fayette, N.Y. He and his increasing number of followers moved on to Ohio, then Missouri, and finally settled in Illinois.

It was in Illinois that Smith declared his intention to run for the Presidency of the United States. It was his order to his followers to destroy the printing press of a newspaper hostile to him that led to his imprisonment

MANCHESTER, NEW YORK STATE
(Ontario County)

and that of his brother Hyram. On 27th June 1844 a hostile mob attacked the prison and murdered Joseph Smith and his brother. The Mormons declared Smith a martyr and Brigham Young took over the leadership of the church. Each year thousands of Mormons from across the world travel to Manchester, New York State, to attend America's largest outdoor pageant which celebrates Smith's finding of the Golden Plates. A golden statue of Moroni, the son of the prophet Mormon, now stands on Cumorah Hill. It was Moroni, according to Mormon beliefs, who guided Smith to find the plates.

Transport links

Road   Off State Highway 90 south east of Rochester (22 miles).

Air   Rochester (Monroe County Airport 22 miles) for local flights, Syracuse (Hancock International Airport, 55 miles).

Climate: No specific figures available. Cool winters, hot summers.

Local press The Daily/Sunday Messenger, Tel (716) 394-0770.

Zip Code   14504

Information via Internet

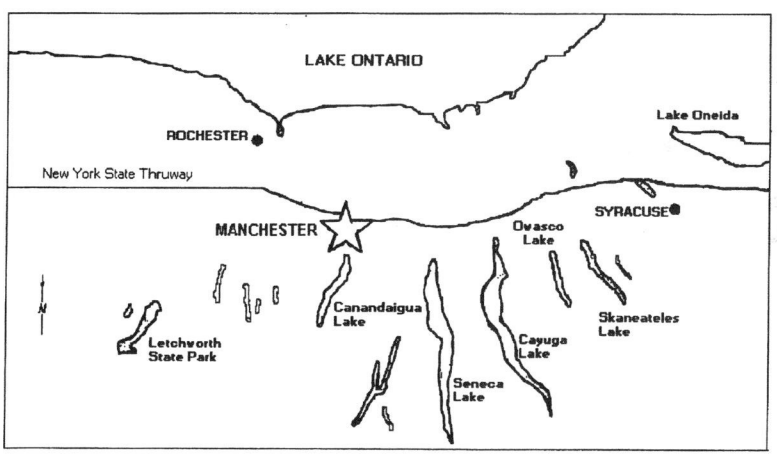

Manchester in the aptly named Finger Lakes
region of New York State

MANCHESTER BRIDGE, NEW YORK STATE
(Dutchess County)

Location   Latitude 41.41N. Longitude 73.51 W.
           On Highway 55 near Arlington.
One of the most elusive of all the Manchesters! The US Government Information Service provides a name and location but nothing further. Repeated letters and emails failed to produce one iota of information. However, the Internet finally came up trumps in the form of an Excite map showing Manchester Bridge to be exactly as its name implies – a bridge over a tributary of the Hudson River. Close by is Manchester Old Road which implies that a former Manchester lurked nearby!

Elevation   181 feet above sea level.
Zip Code   14504
Local press   Poughkeepsie Journal, 85 Civic Center Plaza,
               Poughkeepsie, NY 12601.
Also in New York State - Manchester Corners (Otsego County) – a locality.
Information via Internet

MANCHESTER, NORTH CAROLINA
(Cumberland County)

Location   Latitude 35.11N. Longitude 78.59W.
           Off State Highway 24. Near Fayetteville and Spring Lake.
Population Below 100.

North Carolina, if not especially the very small village of Manchester, has many claims to fame, not the least being that the first English colonists to the New World settled in the area and the Wright Brothers made their famous first flight not far from present day Manchester.

It was not until the English Elizabethan sailor, Walter Raleigh, was granted a Charter by Queen Elizabeth 1 to establish a colony in "Virginia" (now North Carolina), that the first permanent settlement of Europeans was attempted. Raleigh himself did not lead the expedition but sent his cousin, Sir Richard Grenville, at the head of 108 colonists, to establish the first English colony in the "New World". Grenville was immortalised by Alfred Lord Tennyson in his ballad "The Revenge", the story of one ship's battle against overwhelming odds.

These pioneer colonists set sail from Plymouth in 1585 but failed to establish a viable settlement. The survivors were rescued and taken back to England in 1586 by another famous English sailor, Francis Drake.

A further attempt to found a colony was made in 1587 when 110 settlers, including 17 women and 10 children, set sail from Plymouth under

MANCHESTER, NORTH CAROLINA
(Cumberland County)

the leadership of John White. They landed on Roanoke Island where they found the houses of the ill-fated 1585 expedition still standing. White's colonists also suffered extreme privations and White was prevailed upon to return to England the following year to obtain desperately needed supplies. Because of the war with Spain he was unable to return to the new colony until 1590 when he found the settlement deserted and no trace of the colonists apart from the word *"CROATAN"* carved on a tree. No satisfactory explanation of the fate of the lost colonists has been put forward.

Little is recorded as to the origins of Manchester in Cumberland County. The first European settlers, including many Scottish families, arrived in the Little River area in the mid to late 1700's. Descendants of one of the pioneering families, the McCormicks, still live on the land they originally settled. John A.Oates, in his "Story of Fayetteville", gives the name Manchester as coming from "an old manufacturing village on lower Little River". As the manufacturing concerned was the spinning and weaving of cotton it is reasonable to assume that the name derived from Manchester, England, which was the leading importer of raw cotton from the plantations of the southern states.

Many of the mills in Cumberland County were established in the 1850's, the one in Manchester owned by the Murchison family being known unsurprisingly as Manchester Mill. In its heyday the mill worked 1900 spindles and 55 plaid looms, (the Scottish connection?), the Little River supplying the necessary waterpower. This was later supplemented by a steam engine installed in the mid century by Berry Davidson, a millwright. The road from Manchester to Fayetteville is known as Murchison Road to this day. Records also show that in 1863 a Mr. D.L.Livett owned a factory in Manchester for the manufacture of bobbins. The Cape Fear and Yadkin Valley Railroad served the mills of the town for the transport of raw materials and finished goods, and it is likely that Robert Stephenson and Company in England built some of the engines on this railroad. All the stockholders in the railroad lost their investment in 1895 when the company was sold by auction to pay off debts.

Amongst the early settlers in Manchester was the McDiarmid family, originally from the Isle of Islay (famous for its whisky!) off the west coast of Scotland, who settled on the upper side of Little Lower River in the late 1700's. In 1840, in an argument with Ben Atkins, one of the McDiarmid sons was shot and killed. Atkins lived in Lillington, on the other side of the river, and it is not known if he was held to account for the killing. However, in the 1850's when the boundaries of the new Harnett County were being drawn, the McDiarmids objected to their land being in the new county,

MANCHESTER, NORTH CAROLINA
(Cumberland County)

possibly because it would bring them more into contact with the Atkins. Out of deference to their wishes the boundary committee settled the bounds so that the McDiarmids (and hence Manchester also) would remain in Cumberland County.

The McDiarmids, in time, became wealthy plantation and slave owners as indicated in their 1854 "List of Taxables". This showed them to have *"66 black polls (slaves), 1 white, 17 separate tracts of land totalling over eighteen thousand acres, watches of gold and silver, one piano forte, silver plate, one carriage, one rockaway (cradle), one buggy"* and so on. Much more interesting than a present day tax return!

The defeat of the South in the Civil War was followed by years of economic hardship throughout the former Confederacy. The town of Manchester, although incorporated in 1895, did not escape the effects of the war and the subsequent decline of the cotton industry. The mills gradually closed and the workers moved on. In 1919 the US Army purchased large tracts of land in Cumberland County to enlarge Fort Bragg and this army base has continued to expand over the years. The general store and post office closed and eventually all that remained of the once thriving small town was the church and a few houses.

One present day link with the Scottish ancestry of many of the local inhabitants is the annual kirkin, when local citizens wear their clan tartans to church in Longstreet where many of the first settlers are buried. The church is now within the Fort Bragg reservation and only opened to the public once a year for this special purpose.

With the twentieth century came the age of the car and the freeway bringing greater mobility of labour which, in turn, hastened the decline of many small American towns such as Manchester. A "Manchester Township" is still listed as a County sub-division (pop.31,170) in the 2000 US Census but townships, at least in this part of North Carolina, no longer function as local government administrative units. The present town of Manchester is little more than a hamlet which time and the march of progress have all but passed by.

Transport links
Road   On State Highway 24 north of Fayetteville.
Air   Fayetteville (15 miles).
Climate   Hot summers, mild winters.
Elevation   150 feet above sea level.
Local press Fayetteville Observer-Times, 458 Whitfield Street,
            Fayetteville, NC 28306.
Zip   n/a

MANCHESTER, NORTH CAROLINA
(Cumberland County)

Reference   "The North Carolina Gazetteer" William Powell (Univ. NC.).
"The Story of Fayetteville and the Upper Cape Fear" - John A.
Coates.
Also in North Carolina – Manchester, an administrative sub-division of
Mecklenburg County.
Information provided by Bruce Tindall (via Internet); Patricia F. Ferguson,
Librarian, Cumberland County Public Library and Information Center;
Kathryn Y. Lewis, Cumberland County Historical Society.

MANCHESTER, SOUTH CAROLINA

No populated Manchesters have been found in South Carolina but the
name lives on with two Manchester Schools, Manchester State Forest
(Sumter County) and Manchester Creek (York County).

OHIO

Uniquely Ohio lays claim to three Manchesters, two in the northern
part of the State and one in the southern. All are small communities typical
of the many thousands of small towns in America founded by the early
pioneers. To many Americans these small towns are the backbone of the
country, peopled by descendants of the early settlers and still retaining many
of their original pioneering characteristics.

MANCHESTER, NORTHERN OHIO
(Summit County)
"One of the most unusual small towns in Ohio"

Location   Latitude 40.56N. Longitude 81.34W.
Ten miles south west of Akron, near Portage Lakes State Park.
Population   Below one hundred
Lying across the main road from Akron to Canal Fulton and
Massillon, the village of Manchester was first laid out in 1815 by Aaron and
Mahlon Stewart. It flourished from the start, soon rivalling nearby Clinton as
the fastest growing village in the county. In addition to the early English
pioneers (from whom presumably the town name was derived), German
settlers arrived and church services were held in both languages. It is reputed
that President Garfield made frequent visits to Manchester to talk in the
Church of Christ, of which he was member, and that President McKinley
once stayed in the town's hotel. Shades of Queen Elizabeth I slept here!

MANCHESTER, NORTHERN OHIO
(Summit County)

However, when the Fulton canal by-passed Manchester, three miles to the east, it seemed that the village would lose trade and decline. Although many of its early settlers did move on, the discovery of coal deposits nearby revived the fortunes of the village. The mining of coal continued to the late 1920s when the last mine was closed. With the closure of the mines Manchester declined to the sleepy, small village it is today with one store, a summer restaurant and a volunteer fire department. Many of the present day residents are descendants of the original pioneer settlers but they are now obliged to commute to Akron and Clinton for work and services.

Transport links:

Road   One mile east of State Highway 21.
Air: Cleveland (35 miles), Hopkins International Airport.
Climate: Abundant rainfall. High but not oppressive summer
             temperatures, cool to cold winters.
Elevation   1111 feet above sea level.
Local press The Beacon-Journal, 12 E. Exchange St., Akron, OH 44308.
Zip   98353
Reference   "Akron and Summit County, Ohio 1825-1928" Ed. Scott Dix
             Kenfield (Source Akron Summit County Public Library).

Also in Northern Ohio - Manchester Bridge (Noble County); Manchester School (Auglaize County) - historic school; Manchester Township (former administrative area) Morgan County.

Information provided by Steven Hawk, Akron Summit County Public Library.

MANCHESTER, SOUTHERN OHIO
(Adams County)

Location   Latitude 38.41N. 83.36W.
             On the Ohio River overlooking the hills of Kentucky.
Population   2,140

Manchester was the first European settlement in Adams County and the last stockaded village in the State of Ohio. Nathaniel Massie, a surveyor from Virginia, first settled the Manchester locality early in 1791. The site he chose for the new village was at a point on the Ohio River known to the early pioneers as Three Islands, a convenient river crossing. He offered the first twenty five persons who would join him in establishing a settlement one inlot (within the town boundary) and one outlot and a further one hundred acres in the area of the new settlement. Thirty people took up his offer and by March 1791 the settlement was in being and enclosed by a stockade as a

MANCHESTER, SOUTHERN OHIO
(Adams County)

protection against the frequent Native American attacks. Massie named the new settlement Manchester after his hometown in England. Gradually the town developed and houses were built outside the stockade but adjacent to it as these were pioneering days and the stockade would offer some protection in times of danger. A log cabin school was started in 1794 and the first court was held in 1797 in McGate's Tavern. By 1799 the first store had opened, a post office in 1801 and the first brick house completed in 1807.

The settlement's position on the banks of the Ohio River was to play a significant part in the development of the town and it became an important steamboat landing on the route between Portsmouth and Cincinnati. The first steamboat to call at the new landing stage was the "New Orleans" in December 1811. Early small-scale manufactures in the town included boat building, cooperage, pottery, saw mill and furniture. Various retail outlets opened as the town developed and, by the middle of the 19th century, the town was well established with its own bank, churches of various denominations, mayor and town council. The town's first newspaper, "The People's Intellegencer" began publication in 1852, later newspapers being "The Manchester Signal" (still published today as "The Signal"); "The Manchester Gazette"; "The Manchester Herald" and "The Manchester Independent"

The town has been subject to periodic severe flooding from the Ohio River, a particularly disastrous flood occurring in 1884 in which most of the town was under water for ten days. Two major fires in 1859 and 1906 also destroyed many of the older settlement buildings.

Today Manchester, Southern Ohio, remains a small town typical of many in America. Apart from the service sector, main employment is in agriculture, men's clothing and refrigerator parts.

Transport links
Road   On US Federal Route 52. Cincinnati 60 miles.
Air   Nearest airport - Greater Cincinnati International.
Water   The Ohio River links the town with Cincinnati to the west and Portsmouth to the east.
Climate   Average temperatures - Summer 74.7F, winter 33.2F.
Elevation   827 feet above sea level.
Local press The Signal, Ed. William G. Woolard Jr.,
            414 E. Seventh St., Manchester, Ohio, Y51YY.
            The People's Defender, Ed. Herb Lay, 229 N. Cross St., West Union, Ohio, Y5693.
Zip   45144

MANCHESTER, SOUTHERN OHIO
(Adams County)

Reference   "Historical Notes from Manchester Historical Society, Manchester 1791-1991" compiled by Florence Howland.
Also in Southern Ohio - Manchester Township (former administrative area in Adams County).
Information provided by Florence Howland, Manchester Historical Society.

WEST MANCHESTER, SOUTHERN OHIO
(Preble County)

Location   Latitude 39.54N. Longitude 84.37W.
East central Ohio, close to the Indiana border, eleven miles north of Eaton. On US Federal Highway 127 six miles north of US Interstate 70.
Population   433

Although there was an earlier settlement at Hagerstown, a mile to the northeast, West Manchester owes its existence to the coming of the Dayton and Western Railroad. The line opened in 1853 and a railroad halt, about a mile south of Hagerstown, quickly attracted settlers. This halt was to become West Manchester. The town, founded by Otho Brumbaugh, S.G.Landis and J.Studybaker, was platted (laid out in lots) in May 1853. A railway office, depot and warehouse formed the nucleus of the new settlement. In December, 1855, the post office was transferred from Hagerstown to West Manchester, which by then had several businesses established including grocery, dry goods, drugs, tin ware and a harness store.

There appears to have been some crisis of identity in those early days for the town changed its name several times. Named West Manchester in 1855, it became Oderkirk in 1888 and West Manchester again in 1889. There is no record of why the name Manchester was chosen but the prefix west was probably added to distinguish the town from the other Manchester in Adams County, Southern Ohio. By 1875 the population had reached 152 mainly engaged in providing services for the surrounding farming area. By this time the town had its own churches, school, and the lodges of two secret societies, Odd Fellows and Red Men. A town fire department was organised in 1890 and in the first town bank opened in 1897. The town was incorporated on the 1st October 1900, by which time the population had reached 390 persons.

The onset of the Twentieth Century saw the coming of gas lighting (1913), and an automobile garage (Geeting's Auto Inn, 1914). The cars were delivered in pieces by railroad to be assembled by local mechanics. The telephone arrived but local citizens did not like to use the service after nine o'clock at night, apart from emergencies, for fear of waking the operator!

WEST MANCHESTER, SOUTHERN OHIO
(Preble County)

West Manchester has remained a small village though changed in character in recent years. Supermarkets have replaced older stores and the village has a bank, post office, library and community swimming pool. Improved road transportation has brought Dayton and other larger towns within easy reach. The closure of the railroad in the 1980's inevitably altered the pattern of local business but agriculture (hogs and pigs, soya beans, corn and dairy) remains important.

WEST MANCHESTER

1883 - 1983

"Those were the days!" – West Manchester celebrated its Centenary in 1983. (Picture from cover of Centenary Booklet)

Transport links
Road	On Us Federal 127 six miles north of Interstate 70.
Climate	Abundant rainfall with high but not oppressive summer temperatures with cool to cold winters. Annual rainfall 40 inches; snowfall 25 inches.
Elevation	1093 feet above sea level.
Local press	The Register Herald, 542 N. Barron St., Eaton, OH 45320.
Zip	45382
Reference	"West Manchester 1883-1983" Preble County District Library. "Preble County Ohio" Eds. Ione Sell Hiestand, Audrey Shelton Gilbert, Preble County Historical Society, 1992.

87

WEST MANCHESTER, SOUTHERN OHIO
(Preble County)

Reference   "History of Preble County, Ohio" H.Z.Williams & Bro.1798 &
1881(Preble County Historical Society Library).
Also in Southern Ohio - Manchester Township (Morgan County) - former
administrative area.
Information provided by Polly C. Kronenberger, Preble County District
Library and Virginia Lindsey, Eaton-Preble Chamber of Commerce.

MANCHESTER, OKLAHOMA
(Grant County)
"Ride like Hell and Stake a Claim"

Location   Latitude 36.59 N. Longitude 98.02 W.
On Highway 132 on border with Kansas. Very small and
isolated. Enid 38 miles, Oklahoma City 100 miles.
Population   104

Until the latter part of the 19th century most of Oklahoma remained
under Native American control which is known as the Indian era. Cherokee,
Chickasaw, Choctaw, Creek and Seminole, the "Five Civilised Tribes",
settled in the area in the mid 1830's. White settlement was forbidden by law,
although a large tract of land known as the Cherokee Outlet was used for
cattle grazing by Kansas's ranchers with the agreement of and payment to
the Cherokees.

In 1889 Oklahoma was opened to white settlers and the famous
"Cherokee Strip Run" took place on 16th September 1893. Thousands of
would be settlers lined up at three starting points on the Kansas border, ready
to "ride like hell" to stake out a claim in the newly opened territories. It is
said that at each start point the crowd stretched as far as the eye could see.
On the stroke of noon the starting signal of a single gunshot rang out and the
great wave of pioneers, on foot, on horseback and in all manner of vehicles,
rushed forward into Oklahoma. Once a settler had put down a marker with
his name on his "claim", about 160 acres, he then had to file the claim with
the nearest land office. That done, the land was his provided he lived on the
claim and paid for it at the end of five years at a price of $1.50 per acre.

A number of sites for towns were selected in the new territories and
the site chosen for the (Grant County) town that was to become Manchester
was at the terminus of the Hutchison and Southern Railroad on the State line.
The site had been surveyed in the May of 1893 in readiness for the opening
up of the Cherokee Strip. No record exists as to why the name of Manchester
was chosen. Certain lots were reserved for a school and other public
buildings, but other lots were offered free, with free water to anyone who

MANCHESTER, OKLAHOMA
(Grant County)

would start a business. By January 1894 the new town of Manchester had over forty buildings erected and its own newspaper, the "Manchester Journal".

Manchester became what in England would be called a market town, serving the needs of the surrounding agricultural area. The farmers brought their produce and livestock into town to sell and to obtain supplies of lumber, coal, dry goods, groceries, etc. Thus, Manchester developed into a typical mid-west small town, the heart of "real" America, and remained so until the second half of the twentieth century. Local men and women went to do their duty in both world wars, some making the ultimate sacrifice on behalf of their country. Wives and families kept the farms and businesses going while their men folk were away as they always have throughout the ages.

However, with the passing of time came changes, particularly in transportation. The automobile and improved roads brought much greater mobility. This enabled farmers to look further afield for their markets and supplies and, as a consequence, Manchester declined in importance. Today, to quote the words of my friend and correspondent in Oklahoma, Elmer Wood, "all that is left of Manchester is its spirit. Very little remains of the physical portion of the town."

Transport links
Road   On Highway 132 due east of US Interstate 35 (40 miles).
Air   Enid 38 miles; Wichita (Kansas), 55 miles.
Climate   No specific figures available. Generally mild winters, hot summers with great temperature fluctuations.
Elevation   1277 feet above sea level.
Local press The Manchester Journal.
Zip   73758
Reference   "History of Manchester" Elmer Wood.
Also in Oklahoma - Manchester Square Shopping Center, Tulsa.
Information provided by Elmer Wood, Tulsa, Oklahoma.

MANCHESTER, OKLAHOMA
(Grant County)

Once a thriving town but now nearly deserted
Manchester, Oklahoma - looking west along Main Street
(Picture courtesy of Elmer Wood)

MANCHESTER, PENNSYLVANIA
(York County)

Location   Latitude 40.03 N. Longitude 76.43 W.
Eastern Pennsylvania. On Highway 181, off State Highway 83
York 6 miles, Harrisburg 17 miles.

Population   Manchester Township 12,700; East Manchester Township 5078; West Manchester Township 17,035; Manchester Borough 2350.

The first Europeans reached this part of Pennsylvania in the early eighteenth century. They found a well-watered land thickly forested with dense growths of oak, hickory, ash and chestnut. The nearby Conewago Creek and Susquehanna River provided excellent fishing for the Native Americans. The first settlers were English Quakers soon followed by German emigrant farmers.

The writer's namesake, Thomas Cookson, the deputy surveyor of Lancaster County, laid out the site for Manchester Township in 1742. As some of the Quakers came from Manchester, England, it is reasonable to assume that they named the new township after their hometown. The original township area was quite extensive before being reduced to near its present

MANCHESTER, PENNSYLVANIA
(York County)

size in 1848. By this year it boasted of some 300 inhabitants, the population growing nearly five fold over the next thirty five years to reach 1465 in 1783, with 267 houses, 218 barns and 21 mills. The town was sub-divided in 1799 to create the township of West Manchester leaving 350 "taxable inhabitants" within Manchester proper.

In England the cities of Manchester and Liverpool, about thirty-five miles apart, have a history of commercial rivalry stretching over two centuries. Perhaps an echo of this found its way into Manchester Township when, in 1814, William Reeser purchased a tract of land in the centre of the township. His purchase included the area of convergence of several different local wagon and pathways with the York and Conewago turnpike road. Reeser appointed General Jacob Spangler, of nearby York, to survey and plan a new town at this central point. The plan was inscribed "A plan of the town of Liverpool situated in Manchester Township" Why Reeser chose the name Liverpool for his new town is unknown.

In 1815 the area was set out into one hundred numbered lots and tickets sold at $100 to draw a lot - a common custom at the time. Reeser is said to have made a profit of $4000 as a result of this sale.

The town continued to be known as Liverpool until it was incorporated under the name of Borough of Manchester (as distinct from Manchester Township) in 1869. Its post office had long been called Manchester Post Office as the name Liverpool Post Office had previously been granted to a town of that name in Perry County. Manchester Borough was a separate political entity to Manchester Township. At the Borough Election in 1885 there were 135 voters in a total population of 630.

Modern technology came to Manchester in 1891 when the Bell Telephone Company installed lines through the borough. The town council charged the company $1 for each pole within the borough boundary and $2.50 for each mile of line. However, as electric power did not arrive until 1904, the residents had to wait until 1909 before they had their own telephone service. The streets were lit just after the turn of the century when also a street railway (tramway) was constructed.

The original Manchester Township has, over time, subdivided into four – the townships of Manchester, West Manchester, East Manchester and the Borough of Manchester. They surround York City and form the Greater York area. Many township residents commute to work in the city. York County is predominantly agricultural, whilst Manchester Borough (the original Liverpool) remains a typical small American town.

MANCHESTER, PENNSYLVANIA
(York County)

Transport links
Road   On Highway 181 off US State Highway 83.
Air   Capital City Airport, Harrisburg, 17 miles.
Climate   No specific figures available. Warm summers, cold winters, moderate rainfall.
Elevation   492 feet above sea level.
Local press York Daily Record, 1225 George St., York.
Zip   17345
Reference   "Encyclopædia of Pennsylvania" Somerset Publishers, c1983.
            "The Columbia Lippincott Gazetteer of the World", Columbia University Press.
Also in Pennsylvania - Manchester (Allegheny County) - a locality and the historical Manchester Schoolhouse (Washington County).
Information supplied by Gerald Bruce, Lancaster County Library; Shannon Christman, Martin Library; Thomas E. Donley, York County Chamber of Commerce and David Raver, Manchester Township Manager.

MANCHESTER, SOUTH DAKOTA
(Kingsbury County)

Location   Latitude 44.22N. Longitude 97.43W.
            Off US Federal Highway 14, near De Smet.
Population 109

South Dakota will be familiar to all film devotees as its history has provided the basis for countless Hollywood western films, many of which were filmed on location in the state. The Black Hills Gold Rush in the 1870's, and the Indian Wars that didn't end until after the massacre at Wounded Knee in 1890, led to lawless and turbulent times. Hollywood re-enacted and elaborated on them all, from Doris Day as Calamity Jane (real life Mary Jane Canary) singing "The Black Hills of Dakota" and the "Deadwood Stage" to numerous films about Wild Bill Hickok who was shot dead whilst playing poker in Deadwood, a town in South Dakota. The hand he held at the time - a pair of eight's and a pair of aces - became known as the "dead man's hand". Both Hickok and Calamity Jane are buried at Deadwood.

The first white men in South Dakota were the La Verendrye brothers who visited the area in 1742 and claimed it for the King of France. To substantiate their claim they buried a lead plate to this effect on the banks of the Mississippi river, not all that far from the site of Manchester. Apart from the occasional fur trader there was little European interest in the region,

MANCHESTER, SOUTH DAKOTA
(Kingsbury County)

possibly influenced by the fierce inter tribal wars between the Sioux and the Arikara. The first recorded permanent white settler was Pierre Dorion, a fur trader who married a Sioux woman in 1780.

The region became part of the United States as a result of the famous Louisiana Purchase from France in 1803 which opened up the territory to Europeans. However, it was not until the 1870's with the Black Hills Gold Rush and the coming of the railways that the large scale white settlement took place. This led to more conflict between the Native Americans and the new white settlers that did not end until the death of Chief Sitting Bull and the massacre at Wounded Knee in 1890.

First settled in 1882, present day Manchester was originally called Fairview because of its outlook, the name being changed to Manchester for a family of early settlers. Repeating the history of many other small towns it is probable that Manchester owes its existence to the coming of the railroad, sited as it is at a rail halt and passing point on the railroad to Huron and Pierre, the State capital.

Today Manchester is much as it always was, a small American town adjacent to a railroad track and highway. The Township of Manchester is the former administrative area in which the historic Manchester Post Office is located.

Transport links
Road   US Federal Highway 14.
Rail   On line to Huron and Pierre (disused?).
Air   Huron (14 miles).
Climate   Average temperatures: Winter 21.2F. Summer 66.1F.
            Average rainfall: 20.04 inches.
Elevation   1536 feet above sea level.
Local press Huron Plainsman, 49 Third St., Huron, SD 57350.
Zip   57231
Information USGIS via Internet

MANCHESTER, TENNESSEE
(Coffee County)
"The County Seat of Historic Coffee County"

Location   Latitude 35.28N. Longitude 86.05W.
Central southeast Tennessee. Nashville 64 miles,
Chattanooga 69 miles.

Population   8294

In 1763, land speculators, headed by Judge Richard Henderson, purchased vast tracts of land in central and eastern Tennessee from the Cherokee Native Americans. Henderson then employed the famous scout Daniel Boone to find a trail through the Appalachian Mountains to the Kentucky River – the Wilderness Trail. Following this trail, settlers moved into what is now the Nashville area and the European settlement of what is now the State of Tennessee began in earnest.

The pioneer settlers reached the Coffee County area by the late 18th and early 19th centuries, the first permanent homes (log cabins) being built by the three Patton brothers. A stagecoach "resting place" was established at the halfway point on the route between present day Chattanooga and Nashville. It was an important and busy route and therefore, about 1793, a fort was built at Garrison Fork to protect travellers and settlers from attacks by Native Americans. However, the area did not see any increased settlement until after the conclusion of three Indian treaties in 1819. The new settlers came into the region overland by cart and by riverboat, both the Duck and Elk rivers being navigable.

In 1836 the State Legislature of Tennessee created Coffee County (named after General Coffee) from parts of the existing counties of Bedford, Franklin, Rutherford and Warren. By law the County Seat had to be in the centre of the new county, which created a need for a new township in this position, and thereby the town of Manchester came into being. Two landowners, James Erwin and Andrew Hines, deeded 200 acres as the site for the new town in 1836 and commissioners were appointed by the legislature to divide the land into lots for auctioning. The lots varied in size according to their proximity to the town square, the farther from the square the larger the lot. Those bordering the square were perhaps a quarter acre in size, ample for a town house and vegetable garden.

The town drew its name from Manchester, England, in the hope that water from falls on the Duck River could be used to provide waterpower and so turn the town into an industrial area like its English namesake. Cotton and paper mills were established along the banks of the river but the town did not begin to develop until the coming of the railroad in the 1850's.

The advent of the Civil War in the 1860's saw divided loyalties in the town, which, although predominantly favouring the Confederacy, did have

MANCHESTER, TENNESSEE
(Coffee County)

some Union sympathisers. In July 1863, Yankee soldiers occupied the area and the town suffered during the post war depressions. Many of the early records of the town were lost in the courthouse fire in 1870. The town was incorporated in 1905.

Until the 1960's the local economy was based on agriculture but, in recent years, there has been marked industrial growth and Manchester is now a medium sized industrial town. Manufactures include metal products, clothing (pyjamas, robes, sportswear), interior auto parts and fireplace inserts. The Arnold Engineering Development Center has three thousand employees and has the largest underground test facility in the world. Agriculture and the service sector remain major employers. Town government is by a Mayor and six elected Aldermen responsible for public services. The residents of Manchester enjoy excellent water sport facilities and Old Stone Fort State Park is within the town limits.

Transport links

Road   On Interstate 24, equidistant from Nashville and Chattanooga.

Rail   Served by Caney Fork and Western Railroad spur to CSX Transportation's main line in Tullahoma (11 miles).

Air   Tullahoma (12 miles), Nashville International (64 miles).

Water   Cumberland River (channel depth 9') - nearest port facility Nashville (64 miles). Tennessee River (channel depth 9') - nearest port facility South Pittsburgh (50 miles).

Climate   Mean average temperatures - Summer 71F; Winter 45F. Annual rainfall 58.4".

Elevation   1063 feet above sea level.

Local press The Independent (twice weekly), Manchester Times (weekly). The Tennessean (daily); Nashville Banner (daily).

Zip   37355

Also in Tennessee - Manchester Park (Hamilton County) a locality of Chattanooga and Manchester Hill (Cannon County).

Information provided by Pam Sibbs, Secretary, Manchester Chamber of Commerce, 110 E. Main St., Manchester, TN 37355.

MANCHESTER, TEXAS
(Red River County)

Location   Latitude 33.50N. Longitude 95.09W.
             Northeast Texas, near Oklahoma border. Clarksville 18 miles.
Population   200 in immediate area (estimated)
       Texas was first settled by the Spanish in 1682 and became part of Mexico between 1821-36. European settlers arrived in northeast Texas in the 1830's, some migrating from the State of Illinois and possibly some early pioneers stopped off when travelling the famous Santa Fe Trail from Independence, Missouri, to Santa Fe, New Mexico.

       The settlement that was to become Manchester was originally known as Taylor after one of the early settlers. It was renamed Manchester in August 1880 by the postmaster Joseph. E. Srygley after Manchester, Illinois, the town from which he and many of the early settlers had originated. By 1880 the community had reached 100 souls with their own church, school, mill, gin and several small businesses.

       Over the early years of this century Manchester grew into a typical small mid-western rural town serving the needs of the local farmers, the population reaching 142 by 1936. However, road improvements after the Second World War led to many of its residents moving to larger communities such as the nearby county seat of Clarksville and the population declined to a low of 65 residents. Happily, this has shown signs of a healthy recovery in recent years.

       Today all that remains of Manchester is perhaps a dozen or so houses and a community centre that was once the school. The last store closed in 1994. Pinewoods, which provide limited employment in cutting and hauling, surround the village.

Transport links
Road   On County Highway 195.
Rail   Texas North Eastern Railroad at Clarksville (18 miles).
Air   Clarksville/Red River County Airport. Cox Field,
              Paris (22 miles south west).
Climate   Average temperature 65.8F. ranging from 34F to 94F.
              Annual rainfall 45 inches.
Elevation   460 feet above sea level.
Local press The Clarksville Times, Ed. Ben. Black, Clarksville,
              Texas, 75426.

Also in Texas - Manchester and Manchester Dock, two localities in Houston (Harris County) - famous as NASA Mission Control Centre ("Houston, we have a problem"); also Manchester Brook, a stream in Caledonia County.

Information provided by Gavin Watson, Jr., Clarksville/Red River County Chamber of Commerce, Clarksville, Texas, 75426.

MANCHESTER, VERMONT
(Bennington County)

Location   Latitude 43.10N. Longitude 73.04W.
Southwest Vermont, between the Taconies (W) and the
Green Mountains (E). Includes Manchester Center and
Manchester Depot.

Population   Manchester Village 602; Manchester Town 4180;
Manchester Center 2065.

In 1609 Samuel de Champlain, the famous French explorer and trader described the area as "les monts verts" (the green mountains), later Americanised to Vermont. The beauty and natural resources soon attracted settlers to this part of New England – though the long, cold winters may subsequently have caused some of them to have second thoughts! A group that migrated from New York first settled the present site of Manchester in 1764. It was a natural stopping point for travellers being at an intersection of roads going both north/south and east/west. The first of many inns and hotels to provide food and shelter for travellers was opened before 1779 and the settlement was laid out as a town in 1784.

The early economy was based on the local natural timber resources, farming and the milling of marble quarried in nearby Dorset. The coming of the railroad in 1852 brought Manchester within seven hours of New York and the small town soon became a mecca for summer visitors. Manchester Center, as distinct from Manchester Village, was so called in 1886, when local citizens prevailed upon the Post Office to rename the industrial area, previously known as Factory Point. They thought that the name Manchester Center would present a better image for the tourist trade. The importance of "image" is therefore not a late twentieth century discovery!

By the turn of the century Manchester had many fine cottages, hotels and inns and was well established as a summer resort for the New York gentry. The town's first golf course opened, leading the local poet Sarah Cleghorn to write her famous quatrain reflecting the disparity in lifestyles between the locals and the summer visitors.

> The golf links lie so near the mill
> That almost every day
> The labouring children can look out
> And see the men at play

The town now has three 18-hole championship courses but, happily, no mill children! The introduction of winter sports in the mid 1930's had a snowball(!) effect with a marked increase in the number of visitors and the introduction of a regular "snow train" service from New York City.

MANCHESTER, VERMONT
(Bennington County)

The Town Crest of Manchester, Vermont

The First Congregational Church fronted by the Minuteman statue
a landmark in Manchester, Vermont
(both pictures courtesy of the Town of Manchester)

MANCHESTER, VERMONT
(Bennington County)

Today the town is a major all year round sports centre offering a full range of winter and summer activities and some very up market shopping. In addition, visitors come from all over the world to admire the beauty and colour of the autumn foliage on the oak and maple trees. Other attractions include Manchester Village Historic District with its marble sidewalks and over sixty beautiful white wooden 19th century buildings. Hildene, the Georgian mansion built as the summer home of Robert Todd Lincoln, the son of President Abraham Lincoln, is open to the public and retains many of its original furnishings including an Aeolian Pipe Organ.

Transport links

Road	Just north of US Federal Highway 7 and State Highway 7A.
Air	Equinox Airport, Manchester.
Climate	Summers short and moderate, winters long and cold and can be severe. Average summer temperatures 50-60F; Winter 10-20F (-12 to-6C).
Elevation	Varies between 1000 ft. and over 2000 ft. above sea level.
Local press	The Manchester Journal, Memorial Avenue, Manchester Center. Telephone 362-2222; Fax 362-5327. The Vermont News Guide, Box 1265 Manchester, Telephone 362-3535. The Bennington Banner (Daily) 425 Main St. Bennington, Telephone 05201-447-7567.
Zip(s)	05254-5
Reference	"Notes on the History of Manchester" Mary H. Bort. "The Visitor's Guide to Manchester" William Bixby, The Countryman Press, 1985.

Also in Vermont - Manchester Brook (Caledonia County) - stream.
Information provided by Mary H. Bort, RR 1, Box 2085, Manchester Center and Donna Wesley, Town of Manchester.

MANCHESTER, VERMONT
(Bennington County)

Power and skill combined – horsepulls on the 4th July.
Manchester, Vermont
(Picture courtesy of the Town of Manchester)

MANCHESTER, VIRGINIA
(Richmond County)

Location   Latitude 37.31N. Longitude 77.26W
A sub-division of Richmond County but long since absorbed into Richmond (city).
Also in Virginia - Manchester Court (Salem City); Manchester Mill and Manchester Run (a stream in Prince George County); Manchester High School (Chesterfield County).

MANCHESTER, WASHINGTON STATE
(Kitsap County)

Location   Latitude 47.33 N. Longitude 122.32 W.
            Puget Sound opposite Seattle. Bremerton (6 miles).
Population 4958

The first grant of land, in what is now downtown Manchester, was to Isaac C. Ellis who received letters of patent for fifty-three acres from President Ulysses S. Grant on 10th October 1871. By this date a number of loggers, saw mill workers and farmers had already settled in the area. Originally known as Brooklyn, it was renamed Manchester in 1892 in the hope that it would become as prosperous as its English namesake. Lacking roads early travel was of necessity by boat, supplies being obtained from Seattle or from passing boats. A post office was opened in 1893 but almost immediately closed, possibly for lack of a postmaster. The office was not reopened until 1906 when Samuel A. Denniston was appointed postmaster. Denniston and his son also opened a general store in what is now the centre of Manchester.

The building of a small dock in 1908 led to the start of a regular steamship service linking Manchester with Colby, Harper, Southworth and Seattle. The town soon became a popular place for visitors and new families began to settle in the area. A school was opened in 1908, another being needed by 1912. The inauguration of the first car ferry in 1925 brought the need for improved roads which further increased the attractions of the area for tourists and summer visitors. This increase in tourism was not always for the best and in the 1930's the townspeople prevailed on the authorities to close local taverns because of rowdism. In 1940 the Navy Department opened an oil storage base and constructed a dock for naval vessels. This navy facility is still in use today.

The Second World War saw an influx of people into the Manchester area and the school board rented the church basement for use as an additional schoolroom. After the war, new shops and a library were opened and a town fire service was organised. However, the ending of the ferry service in 1949 marked a turning point. In spite of some new development, a new dock was opened in 1967 and a piped sewerage system in 1969/70, the town ceased to grow for a time. In recent years, however, there has been an increase in population and the shoreline from Manchester to Southworth has been densely developed with tiers of homes from the shoreline to the road above.

The town's centenary was celebrated in 1971. Today Manchester still retains much of the original small town charm which first attracted visitors to this rather remote corner of Puget Sound.

MANCHESTER, WASHINGTON STATE
(Kitsap County)

Transport links
Road   Off US State Highway 16.
Water   On Puget Sound. Car ferries to Seattle from Southworth
            (5 miles) and Bremerton (6 miles).
Air   Seattle Tacoma International Airport.
Climate   Cool summers and mild winters.
Elevation   40 feet above sea level.
Local press The Port Orchard Independent.
            The Bremerton Sun.
Zip   98353
Reference   "Manchester" by Louise Hopp
Also in Washington State - Manchester State Park and Manchester
Laboratory Heliport, (Kitsap County).
Information provided by Ms. Judy Peterson, Manchester Library, P.O.Box
128, Manchester, Wa. 98353.

NEW MANCHESTER, WEST VIRGINIA
(Hancock County)

Location   Latitude 40.31N. Longitude 80.34 W.
            Adjacent to the Ohio River in northern West Virginia.
            Near Chester and East Liverpool.
Population "Populated place" according to the US Government
            Information Service but no figure given indicating it to be very
            small. Also known as Fairview and Pughtown.
Transport links
Road   On Highway 8 adjacent to Tomlinson Run State Park.
Climate   Hot summers, cool winters. Average temperatures – Summer
            66F (17C); Winter 34F (1C).
Elevation   1177 feet above sea level.
Local press The Intelligencer, 1500 Main St., Wheeling, WV 26003. Tel.
            (304) 233 0100.
Zip   26056
Information via Internet

MANCHESTER, WISCONSIN
(Green Lake County)

Location   Latitude 43.67N. Longitude 89.06W.
On the Grand River, south east quarter of Wisconsin near Markesan (5 miles).

Population   848

German immigrants were the first to settle the area, a Mr. H.A.Millward arriving in 1846. He subsequently became Justice of the Peace. Mr. Seward came in 1847 and built the sawmill on the banks of Grand River which runs through the town. He also erected the first frame house in the village in 1857. Between 1846 and 1850, Dr. C.R.Hoyt built and opened a store and the schoolhouse and Baptist church were completed. By the third quarter of the century the village had grown to about 100 inhabitants. Fifteen or twenty Welsh families also settled in the south west of the township and formed a small Welsh enclave with their own Chapel and Pastor.

In 1856 the town became known as Manchester, having been previously known as Albany, and later Hardin. The reason for the change is unknown but the most popular conjecture is that male settlers in the surrounding countryside, starved of female company, came to the village chasing women. The town became known for these "man chasers", which, in turn, became corrupted to Manchester. This is a much more interesting explanation than the alternatives offered; that it was named after a settler from Manchester, England, or after a settler named Manchester. A description of the village of Manchester in 1860 reads as follows:

"The village of Manchester is situated near the center of the town(ship), on the high lands north of the valley of the Grand River..... It has about fifty inhabitant; two Stores; one Boot and Shoe Store; one Blacksmith Shop; one Tin Shop; one Wagon Shop; a District School; Post-Office; a Grist Mill, three stories high, two run of stone, capacity, eighty barrels of flour in twenty-four hours..." ("History of Green Lake County" J.C.Gillespie, 1860)

By 1892 the first telephone was installed in the village store and the owner, Mr. George Rhein, constructed a short wave radio which he used to broadcast local news. By this time the village also boasted a hotel, part of which was used for village dances. The original saw mill became a flour and feed mill that was rebuilt after a fire in 1913 and still operates today.

The Wisconsin State Gazetteer, 1919-20, gave the population as 250 and stated: *"Daily stages to Kingston and Markesan, fare 25 cents and to Markesan, 50 cents. Telephone connection."* A stagecoach in the 1920's? In the age of the car and telephone?

MANCHESTER, WISCONSIN
(Green Lake County)

This Manchester remains a small village set in a rural area, being concerned with local agriculture and gravel extraction. It is an area of natural beauty, rolling hillsides and working farms. The town administration comprises of a Town Board, Chairman, Clerk, Treasurer and two Supervisors.

Transport links

Road   On Highway 73-44, 20 miles north east of US Federal 151.
Air   Nearest commercial airports Madison (50 miles) and
              Oshkosh (45 miles).
Climate   Average temperatures - Summer 35C; Winter 6C.
              Annual rainfall 28 inches.
Elevation   670 feet above sea level.
Local press   Markesan Herald, 51 E. John St., Markesan, WI. 53946.
              Fond Du Lac Reporter, Main Office 33 W 2nd St.,
              Fond Du Lac, WI. 53027.
Zip   53945

Also in Wisconsin - Manchester Dam, Manchester Millpond (Green Lake County).

Information provided by Mrs. Harry Friday, Manchester, Wisconsin and Karen Wesse, City Co-ordinator, Markesan.

A house in Manchester, Green Lake County, Wisconsin
Date unknown, possibly early 20th Century
(Picture courtesy of Markesan Chamber of Commerce)

MANCHESTER, WISCONSIN
(Jackson County)

Location   Latitude 44.20N. Longitude 90.78W.
            Between Black River Falls and Sparta.
Population 680
Manchester Township is an administrative area, a municipality within Jackson County. The Black River Falls Community Website describes Manchester thus: - "The township of Manchester was created in 1856 from the Albion Township in south central Jackson County. Manchester has some of the hilliest land in the county with rolling hills in the southern part of the township."

Today the local economy is based around dairy farming and timber, particularly oak.

Transport links
Road   South of Interstate 94 and east of Highway 27.
Climate   Average temperatures – August 82F. January 7F.Can have long periods of extreme cold in winter.
            Annual rainfall 28 inches.
Elevation   n/a
Local press n/a
Zip   54615
Information via Internet

Every star on "Old Glory" could well represent a Manchester in the USA

105

AUSTRALIA

Two stars only for "down under"

As mentioned in the Introduction, it is one of life's mysteries as to why other British place names may be found freely scattered around Australia but not that of Manchester. In spite of my efforts from England and those of my internet friends in Australia, together we have succeeded in tracing only two Manchesters, neither of which is an "inhabited place", one being a lake and the other a square. Coincidentally, as in northwest England, there is a Buxton, and a Liverpool not far from Manchester Square and a Southport near Manchester Lake!

LAKE MANCHESTER
(Queensland)

Location   Latitude 27.29 S. Longitude 152.46 E.
Between Ferndale, Ipswich and Brisbane.

MANCHESTER SQUARE
(New South Wales)

Location   Latitude 34.37 S. Longitude 150.24 E.
A locality about 7km south of Mossvale in Camden County (Parish of Wingecarribee). Post Code 2577.

NEW ZEALAND

"British" place names are generally thin on the ground in New Zealand, many of the original Maori names being retained. Manchester is represented as the name of a homestead in the Otago District at Latitude –45.03, Longitude 169.53, in the foothills of the Dunstan Mountains.

SOUTH AFRICA

South Africa may have its East London, Worcester and Newcastle – and even a Margate – but not, as far as I have been able to discover, a Manchester. However, six farms in the Transvaal are named Manchester which surprised me, it being formerly Dutch territory. As the British and Dutch fought over possession of South Africa at the turn of the twentieth century, it may be that at the conclusion of the war Dutch farms were taken over by British settlers and renamed.

SURINAME

My first indication that the continent of South America may possess a second Manchester came when I was surfing the Internet, attempting to discover further information on the other South American Manchester in Bolivia. For the very few readers who may not be fully familiar with Suriname (Surinam) it is the former Dutch Guiana situated at the north-east of South America, bounded by the Atlantic Ocean to the north, French Guiana to the east, Brazil to the south and Guyana to the west. Suriname is a small country with fewer than half a million inhabitants who live mainly along the coastal plain.

The people are an extraordinary ethnic mix of Asian Indians, Creoles, Indonesian, Chinese and a few Europeans. A very small percentage of the population (3%) is made up of indigenous Native Americans. The interior is heavily forested and mountainous and the climate tropical with annual temperatures between 22.8C and 32.2C.

English traders began to colonise the region in the first part of the 17th century. What was probably the best swap or exchange in history took place in 1667 when the British ceded their part of the region to the Dutch in exchange for New Amsterdam – which later became better known as New York! Suriname had two further short periods of British rule during the Napoleonic Wars, after which it reverted to Dutch control until gaining independence in 1975.

SURINAME

The Geonet Names Server Database on the World Wide Web gives the following information about Manchester in Suriname: -

Location   Latitude 5.53N (also recorded as 5.88N.), Longitude 56.54W (56.90W) Nickerie district.
Population   Populated place – no figure available.
              Very low-lying with an elevation of only 3 feet above sea level.

Manchester is clearly marked on several maps of Suriname e.g. National Geographic, Britannica, Encarta, etc. but I can find no mention of a Manchester in any of the very few reference books available on Suriname, nor on the Internet. An appeal on the Suriname website for information elicited no replies.

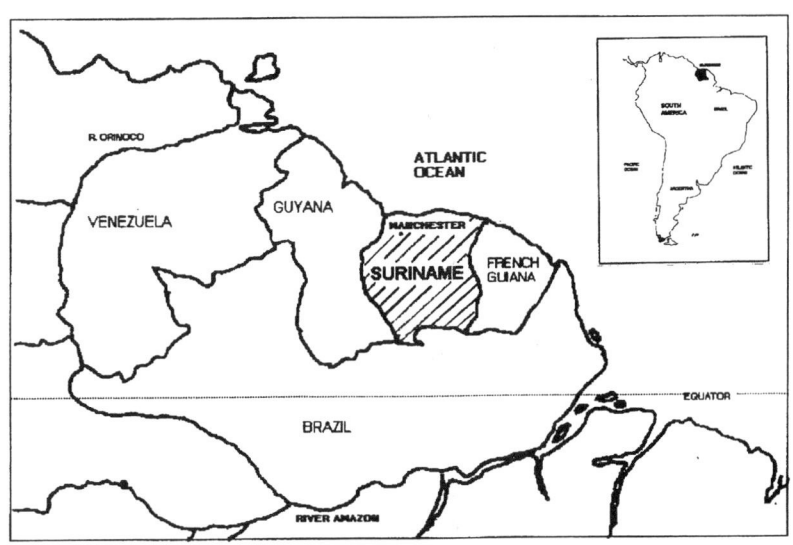

SURINAME –showing the location of Manchester

ZIMBABWE

As with South Africa, I have been unable to trace any towns or villages in Zimbabwe bearing the honoured name of Manchester. However, there is a Manchester farm near Mutare, on the border with Mozambique. Location   Latitude 19.06S. Longitude 32.48E. This location provided by the Geonet Names Server on the Internet.

"LOST" MANCHESTERS

There are many towns and villages which were once known as Manchester but which have been renamed. Perhaps they should more accurately be referred to as "former" or "ex" Manchesters but I find the term "Lost" more appealing. It implies that one day they may be "found" again, their citizens belatedly realising the error of their ways and rejoining the world wide family of Manchesters. Almost inevitably, all but one of the Lost Manchesters are in the United States, the sole exception being in Canada, though I have the feeling that there are undiscovered former Manchesters lurking in Australia and New Zealand.

In the USA settlements often changed their names to avoid confusion with another nearby place of the same name (usually at the request of the US Mail Service). Others changed in honour of a local citizen or notable event, and some because the original settlers had moved on and those taking their place came from a different part of the Old World. Of the ten Lost Manchesters I have discovered in the USA two stand out by virtue of being widely known beyond the shores of the United States.

Niagara Falls, New York. One of the most popular places for honeymoons is Niagara Falls, and newly weds from all parts of the world form a large proportion of the visitors to the Falls. Would it be as romantic, I wonder, to spend your honeymoon in Manchester? The original settlement at Niagara Falls, founded in 1806, was named Manchester. It had a chequered early history being captured by the British in the War of 1812 before being returned to American control after the war. It remained known as Manchester until 1848 when the name was changed to Niagara Falls, Niagara being the Native American word for "at the neck" referring to the Niagara River.

Lakehurst, which is included under New Jersey in the main text, hit the world headlines in 1937 when the German airship Hindenburg caught fire on landing with the loss of thirty-seven lives. Lakehurst was known as Manchester until 1897 when it was renamed at the request of the US Postal Service.

Other Lost Manchesters include: -

College Park, Georgia (Fulton and Clayton Counties) founded in 1830, was known as Manchester until 1895 when it was renamed College Park. The renaming followed the opening of a women's college and the Southern Military Academy in the locality. The original small town has grown to a city of over twenty thousand inhabitants.

Eagleville, Tennessee (Rutherford County)

Ebenezer, Mississippi (Coffee County)- formerly Bucksnort, Manchester.

Yazoo City, Mississippi (Yazoo) – see text on page 110.

Kyle, Indiana (Dearborn County)

"LOST" MANCHESTERS

Paterson, New Jersey (Passaic County) – formerly known as Great Falls, Manchester, New Manchester and Totowa. Renamed Paterson after Governor William Paterson, one of the framers of the American Constitution.

Minneha, Kansas (Sedgwick County) – a station on the St.Louis & San Francisco Railroad.

Moylan-Rose Valley Station, Pennsylvania (Delaware County)

Rochester, Ohio (Warren County)

Also **Morton Lake**, Tennessee formerly Manchester Lake and **Man Run**, a stream in Indiana formerly known as Upper Manchester.

Virden, Canada (south-western Manitoba). Originally named Gopher Creek, it was renamed Manchester in 1882 (reason unknown). Later renamed Virden after Scottish home of Lord Mountstephen, some of whose relatives settled in the town.

YAZOO CITY
(Mississippi)

Location: Latitude 32.50N. Longitude 90.34 W.
        On the Yazoo River west central Mississippi, 44 miles north west of Jackson.

Population: 14,550

Although the site was originally known as Hanan's Bluff, the present day Yazoo City was known as Manchester for a short period in its early history. The earliest record of the town site is the granting of a government patent in 1826 for one square mile of land to Greenwood Leflore, the half-French chief of the Choctaw tribe of Native Americans. He in turn sold all the land for ten dollars an acre to a group of businessmen. The land was sub-divided into lots on a grid pattern *"of a size and form to accommodate Merchants and Mechanics with desirable family residences in its vicinity"*. The lots were advertised for sale by auction. An auction held in February 1830 sold 112 lots in one day with prices varying between $75 and $355 per lot. The town was incorporated under the name of Manchester in the same year. Further auctions followed and many lots were resold on, some several times, at generally higher prices than originally paid.

By 1839 the town had become the largest in the county with a population of about one thousand and the citizens felt that Manchester was no longer an appropriate name for such a thriving community. Being in Yazoo County on the Yazoo River it became Yazoo City. The riverfront was the scene of several Civil War battles and the hull of the Confederate ship "Baron DeKalb" can still be seen at low water. In 1904 a disastrous fire

"LOST" MANCHESTERS

destroyed most of the business district but this was quickly rebuilt and now the area is listed on the National Register of Historic Places. Yazoo is an agricultural and trade centre for the surrounding area with some small-scale manufacturing.

Information supplied by John E. Ellsey, Ricks Memorial Library, 310 N. Main, Yazoo City, MS. 39194. Tel: (601) 746-5557.

ADOPTED MANCHESTERS

It is evidence of the original Manchester's reputation as a world leader in textiles and engineering that that the name came to be given by association to other towns engaged in similar activities. For example, the French town of **St. Denis** on the northern fringe of Paris became known as "Le Manchester Francaise" because it was an industrial centre similar to Manchester though on a much smaller scale. Further examples are: -

Liberec, a city in the northern Czech Republic and a centre for textile manufacture since the sixteenth century was once known as the "Bohemian Manchester".

Monchengladbach, North Rhine-Westphalia, Germany was called the "Rhenish Manchester" being a major centre for cotton textile production, clothing and machinery. As was Manchester, England, Monchengladbach was badly damaged by bombing during the Second World War.

Ivanovo, a large city (pop. 482,000 -1990), one hundred and fifty miles northeast of Moscow and capital of the region. It became a major centre for textile manufacture in the nineteenth century earning the sobriquet of the "Russian Manchester".

Juiz de Fora (pop. 385,756 - 1991), in south eastern Brazil has sometimes been called the "Manchester of Brazil", being a major textile centre and other manufactures including knitwear, metal products, dairy and food products.

The French town of **Mezieres** in the Ardennes was almost destroyed during the First World War and the citizens of Manchester adopted the town in recognition of the heroism and sacrifice of the townspeople. Money was raised to rebuild the hospital which was renamed the "Manchester Hospital" and a district in the town is also known as 'Quartier Manchester'.

FAMOUS MANCUNIANS

Strictly speaking a Mancunian refers to a person born within the city boundary, but I have extended the definition to include those unfortunate enough to have been born in nearby "foreign parts", e.g. Stockport or Rochdale or even further afield but who, by close association with the city, may be called "honorary" Mancunians. To do justice to the almost countless number who deserve mention in any record of the great and the good of this fair city would require several volumes, perhaps even small library. The following listing is therefore a personal choice and I am conscious of the injustice I am doing to the many worthy Mancunians whom I have omitted.

JOHN WILLIAM ALCOCK (1892-1919) in 1919 became the first man, together with **ARTHUR WHITTEN BROWN**, to fly the Atlantic non-stop. Alcock was born in Manchester and served in the Royal Naval Air Service in World War I in which the Turks captured him after a bombing raid on Constantinople. After the war he became a test pilot with Vickers Aircraft and in 1919, with Whitten Brown as navigator, he piloted a converted Vickers Vimy biplane bomber between St. John's, Newfoundland and Clifden, County Galway, Ireland. This was the first non-stop flight across the Atlantic Ocean. The flight, which covered 1950 miles (3140 km.), took sixteen hours and twenty-seven minutes. King George V knighted both men for their achievement. Later the same year Alcock was killed in a flying accident in France. There is a striking memorial to Alcock and Brown in Manchester Airport.

ARTHUR JAMES BALFOUR (1848-1930) became Leader of the Conservative Party and Prime Minister (1902 -1905). He served as Member of Parliament for East Manchester from 1886 to 1905. His "Balfour Declaration" in 1917 in favour of a Jewish national homeland in Palestine, which was endorsed at the 1919 Versailles Peace Conference, was a significant milestone in the eventual establishment of the State of Israel.

ROBERT BOLT, the dramatist and screenwriter, was born in 1924 in Sale near Manchester. He attended Manchester Grammar School and Manchester University. He worked as a schoolteacher until 1958 when the success of his first play, "Flowering Cherry", allowed him to become a full time writer. Amongst his many acclaimed plays the most successful was "A Man or All Seasons" which he adapted for the film in 1966. His screenwriting credits include "Lawrence of Arabia" (1962) and "Dr. Zhivago" (1965).

GEORGE BRADSHAW (1801-1853) published the first railway guide in 1839. He was in business as an engraver and printer in Manchester. His "Bradshaw's Railway Timetables" (price 6d) became famous for their accuracy and comprehensive coverage.

FAMOUS MANCUNIANS

JOHN BRIGHT (1811-1889), together with **RICHARD COBDEN** (1804-1865), led the opposition to the Corn Laws through the Anti-Corn Law League formed in Manchester in 1838. These laws kept the price of bread artificially high to the great detriment of the working classes. Both men were gifted orators and both became Members of Parliament leading the campaign for free trade. The **Free Trade Hall** in Peter Street is a permanent reminder of the major role that Manchester played in the struggle to repeal the Corn Laws.

ANTHONY BURGESS (John Anthony Burgess Wilson 1917 - 1993), the world famous author, was born in Manchester, being educated at Xaverian College and Manchester University. A prolific writer, his works include "The Long Day Wanes" (his Malayan Trilogy), "A Clockwork Orange" (1962) and "Earthly Powers" (1980). The film censor's ban on Kubrick's film version of "Clockwork Orange" has only recently been lifted. Burgess also wrote biographies, children's stories and literary criticism.

FRANCES ELIZA HODGSON BURNETT (1849-1924), the famous "American" novelist, was born in Manchester, England, emigrating to America after the Civil War. Her children's books include "Little Lord Fauntleroy" (1886) and "The Secret Garden" (1911)

JOHN BYROM (1691-1763), the son of a Manchester linen draper, wrote the hymn "Christians Awake! Salute the happy morn!" for his daughter Dorothy. He also invented a system of shorthand writing (patented 1742) and published after his death as "The Universal English Shorthand".

JAMES CHADWICK (1891-1974), born near Macclesfield and educated in Manchester, worked with Rutherford on radioactivity. He was awarded the Nobel Prize in 1935 for his work in confirming the existence of the neutron. He built Britain's first cyclotron (atomic particle accelerator) in 1935 and worked on the Manhattan Project (building the first atomic bomb) during World War 11. He was later knighted for his work.

ROY CHADWICK (1893-1947) was born in Farnworth near Manchester and educated at Manchester College of Technology. An aeronautical engineer, he worked with A.V.Roe and Roy Dobson, designing many famous planes including the First World War Avro 504 trainer, the Anson trainer and the Manchester and the Lancaster bombers of the Second World War. He was killed in a test flight crash of his Tudor 11 jetliner prototype after the war.

RICHARD COBDEN (1804-1865) born in Sussex. In 1828 he moved to Manchester to set up a calico printing business. He quickly established himself in the city and was instrumental in Manchester achieving borough status in 1838. Known as the Apostle of Free Trade, Cobden, with John Bright and five other Manchester merchants, founded the Anti-Corn Law

FAMOUS MANCUNIANS

League. He worked so tirelessly for the abolition of the Corn Laws that he neglected his own business and found himself in financial difficulties. He was elected a Member of Parliament in 1841. After the repeal of the Corn Laws a grateful nation presented him with a testimonial of £60,000.

JOHN DALTON (1776-1844) was the founding father of modern atomic theory. In 1793 he came to teach at New College, Manchester and spent the rest of his life in the city. In 1794 he identified colour blindness (which became known as Daltonism) which affected both he and his brother. In 1808 his "New System of Chemical Philosophy" propounded his proportional atomic theory, which was the first to propose the existence of atoms. His work was to lead to the modern periodic table of the elements and to the law of partial pressures of mixed gases known as Dalton's Law. He was awarded the Royal Society's Gold Medal in 1826.

FRIEDRICH ENGELS (1820-1895), the German social and political philosopher, came to England in 1842 to work in his family's cotton factory in Manchester. He based his first book, "The Condition of the Working Classes in England 1845" on his observations in Manchester. He met Karl Marx in 1844 and together they wrote the "Communist Manifesto" (1848). He returned to Germany during the 1848 revolution and took part in the fighting. After the defeat of the revolution he returned to Manchester. He published several more books on the class struggle and edited the 1885 and 1894 editions of Marx's "Das Capital".

CHARLES HALLE (1819-1895), knighted 1888, was born in Germany and studied and worked in Paris as a young man. After the 1848 Revolution, he moved to London and then to Manchester at the invitation of Hermann Leo, a prosperous Lancashire calico printer. Well supported by the foreign business community in Manchester he became conductor and musical director of the Manchester Gentlemen's Concerts. In 1858 he began a series of concerts in the new Free Trade Hall which was the beginning of the world famous Halle Orchestra. The annual Halle Concerts became a musical institution much admired and copied throughout the world. Many of the world's leading conductors including Sir Thomas Beecham, Hans Richter (Halle conductor 1900-1911), Sir Hamilton Harty (Halle conductor 1920-1933), Sir Malcolm Sargent and Sir John Barbirolli (permanent conductor 1943-58) have performed with the Halle

ANN LEE (1736-1784) was born in Manchester and in 1758 she joined the "United Society of Believers in Christ's Second Coming". Sect members were commonly known as "Shaking Quakers" or "Shakers" because of the bodily trembling brought about by their religious fervour. She became a leading member of the sect and was known as Mother Ann or Ann the Word. She and her followers emigrated to the United States in 1774 and founded

FAMOUS MANCUNIANS

the first Shaker community there in 1776 at Niskayuna (Watervleit), New York. The Shaker sect flourished for a time with as many as eighteen communities but declined in the second half of the nineteenth century. Today only a very few elderly members remain.

DAVID LLOYD GEORGE (1863-1945), the famous Welsh Liberal politician and Prime Minister 1916-1922, was born in Chorlton-on-Medlock, Manchester. When David was two years old his father died and the family moved to Wales. He trained as a solicitor before being elected as the Liberal Member of Parliament for Caernarfon. He became President of the Board of Trade in 1905 and Chancellor of the Exchequer from 1908 to 1915, in which capacity he introduced old age pensions and national insurance. He replaced Asquith as Prime Minister in 1916 at a critical time for the Allies in the First World War. He secured a unified command for all Allied forces which was a significant step in the road to eventual victory in 1918. After the war he won a large majority in the 1918 "khaki election" with the promise of "a land fit for heroes". Lloyd George played a major role in the post war Versailles Peace Treaty but his creation of the Irish Free State in 1921 severely divided his party and lost the 1922 election. The Liberal Party never recovered from this defeat. Lloyd George remained a Member of Parliament until his death in 1945.

THOMAS RILEY MARSHALL (1854-1925) was born in North Manchester, Indiana. He was Governor of Indiana from 1909 to 1913 and Vice-President of the United States from 1913 to 1921 under President Wilson. He is perhaps unfairly best remembered for his remark during a Senate debate "What this country needs is a good five-cent cigar." And who could argue with that?

EMMELINE PANKHURST, nee Goulden, (1857-1928), leader of the militant movement for women's suffrage, was born in Manchester, the daughter of a calico printer. In 1889 she founded the Women's Franchise League and in 1903, with her daughter Christabel, founded the Women's Social and Political Union. Emmeline Pankhurst was frequently imprisoned for her militant pursuit of women's suffrage. When in prison she went on hunger strikes and was forcibly fed. Her other daughter Sylvia also supported the fight for votes for women. Emmeline published her autobiography "My Own Story" in 1914. Partial women's suffrage was gained in 1918 and equality with male suffrage in 1928.

FREDERICK HENRY ROYCE founded the firm of Royce Ltd., mechanical and electrical engineers, in Manchester in 1884. He made his first car in Hulme in Manchester, 1904. In the same year he met Charles Rolls, the owner of a London car dealership. In 1906 they formed a partnership in Manchester to produce high quality motor cars and exhibited

FAMOUS MANCUNIANS

their first car, the Silver Ghost, at the Paris Motor Show in 1907. The car, which featured the distinctive Rolls Royce radiator, was an instant success and the company became the world's premier luxury car maker.

LORD RUTHERFORD (1871-1937). New Zealand born Ernest Rutherford was a professor at Manchester University when he was awarded the Nobel Prize for Chemistry in 1908. His research, into the structure of the atom, led to the revolutionary understanding of the atom as a miniature universe in which the mass is concentrated in the nucleus (which he named), surrounded by planetary electrons. He also discovered alpha, beta and gamma rays. After the First World War, during which he worked on methods of submarine detection, he became Cavendish Professor at Cambridge. He continued his research into the atom and radioactivity throughout his life, publishing many scientific papers and books.

ALAN MATHISON TURING (1912-1954) was born in London and became Reader in Mathematics at Manchester University. In 1936 he outlined the concept of a "universal computing machine" (the Turing machine) which foreshadowed the modern digital computer. Turing also worked on the concept of artificial intelligence. During the Second World War he was involved in the Ultra Project that led to the breaking of the top secret German Enigma code. It is only in recent years that his pioneering work on computers and artificial intelligence has received the recognition it deserves.

EDWIN ALLIOT VERDON ROE (1877-1958) was born in Patricroft near Manchester. He received training in railway, motor and naval engineering. At the age of fifteen he went to Canada and assisted in the design of a flying machine. In 1907, after his return to England, he designed, built and flew his first biplane, a year before the first officially recognised flight in England by John Moore-Brabazon. In 1910 he formed the A.V.Roe Company with his brother, Humphrey Verdon Roe. The company designed and produced the famous Avro 500 series of biplanes of which the 504 became the standard bomber/trainer of the Royal Flying Corps in the First World War. The 504 continued to be used for flying instruction for many years after the war and were the first aircraft to be successfully launched by catapult. He sold out the A.V.Roe Company to Armstrong Siddeley in 1928 and formed a new company, Saunders-Roe, to build flying boats. This company built the first jet-powered seaplane, the SR-A1 and the famous Princess flying boats. The AVRO name lived on in the Lancaster bomber of the Second World War and in the post war Vulcan bomber. The highly successful Avro RJ series of regional jet airliners was produced at Woodford near Manchester.

FAMOUS MANCUNIANS

JOSEPH WHITWORTH (1803-1887) was the engineer who introduced the standardised screw thread named after him. Although not strictly a Manchester man, being born in Stockport, in 1833 he set up his own tool making business in Manchester and the venture soon prospered. He developed means of machining to tolerances never before achieved in engineering. This allowed a standardisation so that shafts, bearings, gears and screws could be interchanged. He was a philanthropist who donated large sums of money to education and charity.

MANCHESTER MISCELLANY

ABRAHAM LINCOLN The famous American Civil War President had strong associations with the city through the support that the working people of Manchester gave in the fight to abolish slavery in the American Civil War. Today, from his lofty perch in Lincoln Square, he casts his benign eye on the citizens of Manchester. The statue, completed in 1917, is possibly the best-known work of the American sculptor George Grey Barnard (1863-1938) who was much influenced by Rodin.

THE BRIDGEWATER HALL was opened in 1996 to meet the city's need for a modern, purpose-built concert hall. Costing £42 million, it seats over two thousand people and is home to the Halle Orchestra and the B.B.C Philharmonic Orchestra. Amongst its many outstanding features the Bridgewater has a Marcussen Organ. This "wondrous machine" has over five thousand pipes ranging from 2 inches to 32 feet in length.

THE FREE TRADE HALL. The Free Trade Hall in Peter Street is a permanent reminder of the major role that Manchester played in the struggle to repeal the Corn Laws in the nineteenth century. The first of three Free Trade Halls built on the same site was erected as a temporary wooden pavilion to hold three to four thousand people. The building took one hundred men eleven days to complete. The present (and third) Free Trade Hall was completed in 1851 and became the home of the Halle Orchestra. In the Second World War it was very badly damaged by bombs during the Christmas blitz of 1940. After the war the interior had to be completely rebuilt and the Hall reopened in 1951. It remained the major concert hall for Manchester and the Halle Orchestra until recently when the new Bridgewater Hall opened. There are plans to redevelop the Free Trade Hall as a hotel.

HALLE ORCHESTRA is the fourth oldest symphony orchestra in the world, being founded in Manchester in 1858 by Charles Halle (knighted 1888). Under Halle it became one of the leading orchestras in the world.

MANCHESTER MISCELLANY

Among its many subsequent conductors Sir John Barbirolli is undoubtedly the most famous, being its permanent conductor from 1943 to 1958. Under his direction the Halle regained its reputation as one of the world's leading orchestras and today retains this reputation under the guidance of conductor Mark Elder.

H.M.S. MANCHESTER. The first "Manchester" was a Gloucester class light cruiser that saw considerable action in the Second World War. Launched in April 1937, she was torpedoed in 1941 whilst escorting a convoy to beleaguered Malta. Repaired in Philadelphia she formed part of the escort to the famous "Pedestal" convoy to Malta in August 1942. Off Tunisia she was attacked by Italian torpedo boats. Crippled after being torpedoed and too badly damaged to be saved she was scuttled. One hundred and fifty crew members lost their lives, one hundred and forty five being saved. The current H.M.S. Manchester, a type 42 destroyer commissioned in 1982, serves as a front line ship of the Royal Navy.

MANCHESTER REGIMENT The "Manchesters" have a long and distinguished history. The Regiment was first mustered in 1756 as the 63rd Foot, which was amalgamated in 1881 with the 96th Foot to form the Manchester Regiment. In 1958 they joined with the King's Regiment (Liverpool, 8th Foot) to form the present day King's Regiment (Manchester and Liverpool). The "Manchesters" fought with great distinction in the two World Wars and in virtually every major campaign of the British Army.

MANCHESTER INTERNATIONAL AIRPORT has grown from very humble beginnings to being voted the "World's Best Airport" in 1996 by the International Air Transport Council. Opened in 1938, with a grass landing strip, it became the main armed forces parachute training centre during the Second World War. Reopened to civil traffic in 1946, its development has kept pace with the rapid growth of air transport in the post war years. Over twenty million passengers fly each year from Manchester on scheduled or charter flights. The airport employs some fifteen thousand people and virtually all the world's major airlines have services to and from Manchester. In 2000 a second runway was added which further increased the airport's capacity.

MANCHESTER ART GALLERY Designed by Sir Charles Barry, the architect of the new Houses of Parliament and the Manchester Athenaeum, the Gallery was built in 1834 in the Greek Ionic style. Amongst its many art treasures is a superb Pre-Raphaelite collection and works by Gainsborough, Stubbs, Turner, Ford Madox Brown, William Etty, Holman Hunt, Dante Gabriel Rossetti and many other notable artists. The Art Gallery, including the adjacent Modern Art Gallery, reopened in May 2002, after undergoing major refurbishment. The Whitworth Art Gallery, situated near the Victoria

MANCHESTER MISCELLANY

University, houses important collections of British watercolours, wallpapers, prints and sculpture.

MANCHESTER COLLEGE, Oxford, now Harris Manchester College, was founded in Manchester in 1786 by English Presbyterians to provide higher education for Nonconformists who were barred from entry to Oxford and Cambridge universities. The College moved to Oxford in 1889.

MANCHESTER GRAMMAR SCHOOL was founded in 1515 by Bishop Hugh Oldham (1452-1519?) as the Manchester Free Grammar School It was for Lancashire boys who, *"having pregnant wit have been for the most part brought up rudely and idly"*. Hugh Oldham bought three local mills to provide an income of £29 a year to maintain the school and to provide Foundation Scholarships which are still awarded today to deserving boys. The Bishop's badge and his motto, Sapere aude (Dare to be wise), still feature in the school. Originally sited in Long Millgate in the town centre, the school moved to its present buildings in Fallowfield in 1931. Famous old boys of the school include Humphrey Chetham (1580-1653) and Charles Worsley (1622-1656). Chetham founded the Hospital School in Manchester which still bears his name and is now a world famous school for young musicians. The school is home to Chetham's Library, which is claimed to be the first free library in Britain. Worsley, a supporter of Oliver Cromwell, is credited with removing the mace, "that bauble", the symbol of the Speaker's authority, from the House of Commons in 1653, when Cromwell ordered the Commons to be cleared. He later became Manchester's first Member of Parliament and Major General in charge of Lancashire, Cheshire and Staffordshire.

"THE MANCHESTER GUARDIAN" (**"THE GUARDIAN"**) newspaper founded (and edited) in 1821 by John Edward Taylor and a group of *"respectable and moderate persons of Manchester"*. The paper changed to its present title "The Guardian" in 1959 and the editorial staff moved to London, thus breaking the century old connection with Manchester. Its associated evening paper, the **"Manchester Evening News"** (founded 1868) is the largest regional paper in the country.

THE MANCHESTER SHIP CANAL, opened by Queen Victoria in 1894, was one of the engineering wonders of the Victorian age and made Manchester the world's first inland port. The canal gave ocean-going ships direct access to the heart of the Manchester conurbation for the import of raw materials, particularly cotton, and the export of finished goods. Sixteen thousand men took six years to build the canal at a cost £17 million pounds, a vast sum of money in those days. At its opening the canal was 35.5 miles long, 28 feet deep and 120 feet wide. Five locks lifted ships seventy feet above sea level and the canal soon became the main artery for trade between

MANCHESTER MISCELLANY

northwest England and the rest of the world. The decline of manufacturing in the region, particularly in the cotton industry, and the growth of road transport led to the decline in importance of the ship canal. In the 1980's major commercial and residential development on the site of Manchester docks has further restricted use of the canal.

SPORT - Manchester has so many claims to fame in virtually every sporting activity that each sport would merit a complete chapter or even a book to do full justice to the prowess of its citizens. The city has nurtured numerous Olympic medal winners and, in team sports, the list of trophies won and famous players seems endless. The city is home to two famous soccer clubs, Manchester United and Manchester City, and is host to the 2002 Commonwealth Games. For this latter event a "state of the art" stadium has been built in the east of the city.

RYLANDS LIBRARY In 1890 construction was begun in Deansgate of a new library to house valuable early books and manuscripts. The library took nine years to complete and commemorated John Rylands, one of Manchester's most successful cotton merchants. Now part of Manchester University, the Library houses an internationally renowned collection of rare books and manuscripts.

HIGHER EDUCATION Most cities have a university but Manchester boasts of no less than four within a five-mile radius of the city centre. The Victoria University of Manchester, founded in 1846 as Owen's College, gained University status in 1851. The University of Manchester Institute of Science and Technology (UMIST) began life in 1824 as the Mechanics Institute, gradually developing into the world famous UMIST of today. The two universities, the Victoria University and UMIST, can lay claim to twenty Nobel Prize winners, a truly remarkable record. Manchester Metropolitan University, the baby of the family, was founded 1970. Salford University, which, although in the City of Salford, is a mere stone's throw from Manchester City centre. Salford University began life in 1896 as the Royal Technical Institute, receiving its Royal Charter as a University in 1967. The Duke of Edinburgh was Chancellor of Salford University for many years. In addition to the Universities, the Royal Northern College of Music is world renowned, being founded by Sir Charles Halle in the late nineteenth century.

ODDS AND ENDS

"THE MANCHESTER MADONNA" by Michelangelo - National Gallery, London. An unfinished painting (egg tempera on wood) in which Christ is seen indicating a passage in the book held by the Virgin. The full title is "The Virgin and Child with St. John and Angels" (1495). It became known as "The Manchester Madonna" after being exhibited in the city in 1857. Some authorities have questioned whether the work is by Michelangelo.

TAILPIECE!

MANCHESTER TERRIERS have been bred in the Manchester area, and elsewhere, from about the middle of the nineteenth century. Originally a cross between a whippet and a ratting terrier, they are black and tan in colouring with close, glossy coats. The Standard Manchester terrier is 14 to 16 inches high with the Toy variety reaching 6 to 7 inches. Both are similar apart from size and shape of the ear. Known as the "Gentleman's Terrier" in Victorian times because of their dignified manner, they are intelligent and friendly and make excellent pets.

The Manchester Terrier – sleek, dignified, alert and intelligent.